Struggling Giant

Berkeley College

From the Library

of

ABOUT THE AUTHOR

Kerry Brown first visited China in 1990, before studying Chinese in London, and then Inner Mongolia, China. He worked for the Foreign Office, in London and Beijing, before becoming an Associate Fellow at Chatham House, and setting up Strategic China Ltd. He is the author of *The Purge of the Inner Mongolian People's Party in the Cultural Revolution in China, 1967–1969* and has written about China for Critical Asian Studies, Far Eastern Economic Review, The Liberal, and others. He is currently working on a second book about Chinese investment, which will come out in early 2008.

Also from Anthem Press

Ha Joon Chang *Kicking Away the Ladder*
Anna Di Lellio (ed.) *The Case for Kosova*
Jackie Gower and Graham Timmins (eds.)
Russia and Europe in the Twenty-First Century
Christophe Jaffrelot (ed.) *A History of Pakistan and its Origins*
Claude Markovits (ed.) *A History of Modern India*
Walter G. Moss *A History of Russia, Volumes 1 & 2*
Peter Nolan *Transforming China*
Erik Ringmar *Surviving Capitalism*
Richard Sakwa (ed.) *Chechnya*

Struggling Giant

China in the 21st Century

Kerry Brown
Foreword by Jonathan Fenby

ANTHEM PRESS
LONDON · NEW YORK · DELHI

Anthem Press
An imprint of Wimbledon Publishing Company
www.anthempress.com

This edition first published in UK and USA 2007
by ANTHEM PRESS
75-76 Blackfriars Road, London SE1 8HA, UK
or PO Box 9779, London SW19 7ZG, UK
244 Madison Ave. #116, New York, NY 10016, USA

British Library Cataloguing in Publication Data
A catalogue record for this book is available from the British Library.

Library of Congress Cataloging in Publication Data
A catalog record for this book has been requested.

ISBN-10: 1 84331 278 6 (Pbk)
ISBN-13: 978 1 84331 278 9 (Pbk)

1 3 5 7 9 10 8 6 4 2

Cover photograph: *Shanghai Street* © 2007
Stuart Isett / www.isett.com

Printed in EU

CONTENTS

FOREWORD

Jonathan Fenby

China is at a pivotal point in its modern history. Given its global importance, this has major implications for the rest of the world. But there are serious limitations to the extent to which the rest of the world understands China. Every day seems to bring a new mind-boggling statistic from the People's Republic: foreign exchange reserves are climbing above the trillion dollars mark, China is about to have 400 million mobile telephone users, the city of Chongqing will number more than 30 million people, China is set to become the world's biggest emitter of greenhouse gasses and the largest brewer of beer on the planet.

After a terrible period between the 1850s and the 1970s, China is back on course and set, in Napoleon's phrase, to amaze the world. In the interim, it went through vast rebellions, the fall of the Empire, a decade of warlord rule, a stumbling Republic, invasion by Japan, followed immediately by civil war. Only with the Communist victory in 1949 did the world's most heavily populated nation achieve a stable system – but that was followed by a quarter-of-a century of purges, the Great Leap Forward and the Cultural Revolution before Mao died and Deng Xiaoping introduced something akin to normality at the end of the 1970s.

Whether China can preserve what has been achieved since then, and build upon it, must be one of the major questions of our time. It is a question the world has not really got to grips with. Is China a competitor or a partner? Can long-term relationships be built with a nation which operates on different ideological principles to most of the rest of the globe, and is driven, primarily, by such motors as the overwhelming need for energy, a mercantilist trade policy and an overt rejection of democracy? Is the lure of the China market – Western and Japanese businesses have salivated for decades at the vision of a billion plus consumers – truly the last great market Eldorado on the planet, or is it a snare and delusion in which companies will end up losing their shirts as the Chinese keep the profits for themselves?

There are two simplistic responses. One is to smile optimistically, invoke the growth figures and the way the economy is moving up the value chain and the army of rural workers still waiting to come into the industrial labour force. China, the optimists say, is bound to go on growing. Its problems will work themselves out over time; for instance prosperity and the emergence of a substantial middle class will lead to a new ecological consciousness that will produce solutions to the country's horrific environmental degradation, while China's growing global involvement will lead to a co-operative approach to the competition for energy.

The other extreme is to adopt a doom-and-gloom attitude: the economy will over-heat and blow up, the political system will collapse as the Communist Party proves unable to deal with the challenges facing it, the environment will poison the country, the banks will fail under the weight of bad debts, corruption will sap the regime, China will go to war over Taiwan, provoking a major conflict that could bring down the world economy.

While those two solutions may have the appeal of offering clear-cut answers to the China puzzle, they are both, almost certainly, wrong. Or, rather, they each contain grains of truth, but simplify what is a very complex problem, to which the leadership in Beijing may well not have the answers. A great merit of Kerry Brown's insightful book is that, as well as illustrating and analysing the problems, it lucidly explains why the issues – and the solutions – are so complex. That complexity may make them more difficult to grasp, but it is an essential part of what makes up the China of the 21st century.

This complexity stems from a broad set of factors, ranging from the nature of the system to geography and history. Too many accounts if China today starts as if the PRC had suddenly leaped fully-formed into its new guise with the reform programme Deng Xiaoping launched in 1978. But, to start with, it is impossible to understand China today without taking into account the complexities and lasting impact of the Cultural Revolution of 1966–78, as Dr Brown does in his original and stimulating account of that decade.

China may have changed beyond recognition, at least in the cities and fast-growing regions, but the past always lurks in the background, and sometimes more up-front – Mao's face still looks out over Tiananmen Square and from the postage stamps. Some problems from the recent past remain very much unsettled, notably the 'three ts' – Taiwan, Tibet and the leadership's refusal to come to terms with what happened in Tiananmen Square in the spring and early summer of 1989. Above all, the way China is ruled has to be seen against a long historical inheritance of top-down power modulated by regional particularism.

The economic gamble that Deng Xiaoping undertook in 1979 – that increased prosperity could provide a new legitimacy for the Communist party – was accompanied by a refusal to conduct an equivalent experiment politically. His legacy remains in place today on both counts. In 2007, the Prime Minister made a point of ruling out democracy – village elections have been allowed but they are usually carefully controlled. The top-level political jockeying takes place behind closed doors in the Politburo, not in public, and only becomes apparent to the country much later when an official is sidelined and another promoted. The mass movements of Maoist days are long gone, but the regime still operates on slogans – President Hu Jintao's 'Harmonious Society' being the most recent. On the 110th anniversary of Mao's birth, The President sill extolled him as a model; the official verdict is that only 30 per cent of what he did was bad.

A middle class is rising and growing, but there is little sign of the political awareness and agitation for power-sharing that characterised similar people in Britain and American in the 18th and 19th centuries. Though individual liberty has increased greatly, any group that organises itself and is seen to present a challenge can expect to be repressed. The most serious challenge may lie, rather, at the grassroots where villagers angry to land grabs by officials, taxation, pollution, corruption and local complaints stage regular protests, sometime spilling over into violence. But these are not co-ordinated.

There is no alternative party waiting in the wings with a fresh ideology and an army. So the chances must be that the Communist regime will hold on to power, albeit of a country that conforms less and less to the Communist model economically and socially. Whether the Leninist system can adapt to the circumstances which its leaders have, themselves, altered so radically, and offer effective rule remains a major question but the oft-forecast collapse of the regime seems unlikely, making it all the more important to try to understand what makes it tick.

Equally, one needs to remember quite how large and varied China remains in its geography, its ethnic differences, dialects, cultures traditions. The material progress since the late 1970s has accentuated the gaps between the booming coastal regions and the vast interior – average household consumption in Gansu in the North-west is a third of the level in Zhejiang on the West coast. Shanghai's bright lights seem to belong to a different country to villages without running water and mountainous areas with, at best, primitive roads, or, the traditions, cultures and dialects that mark this continent of a country. As the title to Chapter Two puts it: 'What Do We Mean When We Say China?'

In answering that, one needs to treat official statements, statistics and claims with scepticism. The often fragile relationship between the centre and the provinces has to be put into the balance – Beijing may announce all manner of new programmes, but will provincial leaders implement them and, if they do, will the subordinate officials put them into practice where it counts? The kind of analysis Kerry Brown offers is a very valuable guide on that path. But it is probably safe to say that China will still have plenty of surprises in store for the outside world in the coming years – but also for itself and its leaders.

– Jonathan Fenby

INTRODUCTION

The rise of China will be one of the major issues of the twenty-first century. The impact of this rise will take many generations to absorb. But make no mistake about it, China will be a part of all our lives, and its importance will grow over the years and decades to come. The signs for this are everywhere. They go far beyond the hoary old statistics about its enormous population and geographical size. These belong to the old picture of China we now need to grow beyond. New figures must be attended to. Ones like the fact that China consumes more energy than any other place in the world apart from the US, a jump of over a dozen places in the last decade. China produces more patents than any other country, despite its reputation as an intellectual property violator. It produces over 300 thousand engineers to the UK's 30 thousand per year. Its government has lifted more people out of absolute poverty than any other in history. It has 100 million Internet users, 300 million mobile phone users, and has become one of the world's largest consumers of copper, zinc, gold and lead. China may well be the world's factory, as a previous Chinese Premier Zhu Rongji famously claimed in the 1990s. But it is also lacking in resources. The balance between China as a provider and a taker will be a critical issue for all of us, inside and outside China, over the coming century.

There are sceptics. People who know something of the long history of false dawns portending the coming emergence of China. China's rise, they claim, is in fact a well worn cliché. Over the course of the last 150 years Victorian clothing manufacturers and American insurance salesmen (among them in the 1930s the great Mongolianist and eventual founder of the East Asian Studies department at Leeds University, Owen Lattimore) have all been lured to the Chinese market by the idea that if each one of China's huge population bought just one of their products they would get rich. One of the earliest of these was the journalist turned businessman, Carl Crow, who was active in Shanghai in the early part of the last century, and wrote the 1937 classic *400 Million Customers*.[1] In the 1980s, China was so awash with foreign investment that one writer compared it to a careering Beijing jeep.[2] That jeep ground to a halt with the rude shock of the 1989 Tiananmen Square Incident/Massacre. To the sceptics, there is nothing new under the sun. All that makes the last five years different from those periods of enthusiasm before is simply the length of its stability. And that, they argue, is more down to the benign international environment than because of any internal dynamics in China itself.

They could, with some justice, point to the example of Japan. In the 1980s and early 1990s, Japan was receiving similar plaudits. Japanese management methods, Japanese design and Japanese economic power were feared and admired in equal measure. Walking around the boundaries of the Imperial Palace in Tokyo with an American friend in 1990, they pointed out to me that the value of the real estate within the mundane brick walls we were looking at across the dark lake was worth more than the whole of California. Japan then seemed like a mighty power generator, its people swarming out as businessmen (very rarely women) and tourists, exercising their new consumer power, rattling the cages of the US who regarded their trade practices as threatening.

In 2006, while slowly emerging from the doldrums, Japan presents a humbler story. Still the world's second largest economy, and with some of the world's most respected brands (Toyota has been particularly powerful), it has undergone over a decade of recession and stagnation. Many of the salarymen through whose efforts the Japanese economy was resurrected have been through tough times, losing their jobs, looking for new things to do. Many of the younger generation simply don't buy into their self-sacrificing and punishing work ethic. Japanese management practices would certainly not now be held up as world beating models. They were exposed as inflexible and unimaginative when the crunch really came.

In ten or 20 year's time, then, will we look back on the mid 2000s as the period of over optimism towards China, similar to that towards Japan? Will

---

1   See Paul French, *Carl Crow: A Tough Old China Hand,* Hong Kong 2006. Portentously, Crow was to grow immensely rich in Shanghai during its heyday, and then return to his native US in 1940 with only a suitcase and the clothes he stood in, the rest of his belongings a victim of the Sino-Japanese war raging at the time.

2   Jim Mann, *Beijing Jeep: The Short Unhappy Romance of American Business in China*, New York 1990.

it look like all the other phases before, disrupted by some nasty shock just round the corner which no one noticed coming, and yet everyone in hindsight says they should have seen?

This book approaches the future of China by looking at thematic issues from its recent past. There is, in fact, a mountain of information about China – going back over the last 58 years of the history of the People's Republic of China (PRC). China watchers (a breed I'll talk about later) have been producing enormous quantities of research, analysis and opinions since day one of the PRC. From the monumental *Science and Civilization in China* series project begun under Cambridge scholar Joseph Needham in the 1950s and ongoing to this day, to accounts of life during the period of the great closure under Mao Zedong, and the tidal wave of economic analysis over the last decade, one thing that isn't lacking about China is information, even if the quality and presentation of this is widely variable.

It has to be admitted that a common theme of much of this material before was its partisanship. You were either on the side of the Chinese government and rulers, or you were against them. Their revolutionary aspirations before the 1980s (they after all committed the colossal sum in the 6.5 per cent of Gross Domestic Product (GDP) in the 1960s to assisting revolutionary struggle beyond their shores[3]) unsettled people. It dug into xenophobia and sometimes outright racism. The PRC granted access to only the favoured few, which compounded things. Even today, academic research in and about China is never an easy task. In 2000, a US based, Chinese born scholar was rewarded for his research into the role of Premier Zhou Enlai in the Cultural Revolution (CR) by being banged up in jail for over a year. Despite this, there has been a formidable array of studies, seminars, and documentaries about China, particularly in the last two decades. It's interesting to see what patterns emerge from this about what people were right, and wrong about, when they thought about where China would get to in the early 2000s.

My aim in this book is simple. As a first step I simply present two sorts of futures that China might have in the next 30 years, one where it is stable, the other where it is unstable, to map out the sort of territory we need to think about. In order to decide which of these futures is more likely, I will then look at particular themes and issues that matter when we think about China now. The first question will be the fundamental (but surprisingly hard

---

3   Lowell Dittmer, 'Pitfalls of Charisma', in *The China Journal*, *Australian National University, Contemporary China Centre*, No 55, p 123.

to answer) issue of what we actually mean when we say China. To try to answer that, I look at some of the PRC's recent history, and how this concept of a single nation, both within and outside China, has had different pressures and ideas packed into it so that, today, there are many areas in which 'China' contains some highly paradoxical content.

I'll then embark on a journey through some specific areas to try to understand modern China better. I will look at Chinese politics through the two kinds of languages talked in China today, the language of officials and power holders, and the language of normal people, plotting out the immense disconnect between these. And then, I will look at the real pressure points on China's current development – the massive problems involving its environment, the issue of its highly divided economy, the contemporary crisis of public morals and belief systems and the fault lines between particular constituent parts of China's enormous population, looking at what tensions between these might do to the stability of China as a whole.

My key point will be that, in a way that perhaps wasn't so true before, China matters to us greatly now. In the twenty-first century, China is reaching out. It produces most of the consumer goods we use, which are inextricably linked to the global economy we rely on for much of our prosperity. Its companies are starting to be more visible, its people are already travelling more than ever before. It will no longer occupy a niche minority interest area, as it did for so much of the last few decades. Even relative latecomers like myself (I came to China in my mid 20s, after studying English literature and then working as a teacher in Japan and Australia) can remember the lean, mean years when letting slip you were studying China or Chinese in any way usually elicited a fascinated response, along the lines one would now convey to someone trying to master a dead language like Sanskrit or ancient Persian. We can no longer afford to be China watchers, observing this esoteric and mysterious entity with detached fascination. The new China is part of our modernity, in our houses, on our televisions, the origin of many of the goods we buy, the source of some of the pollution in our air and its children a significant presence in our universities. We need to think about China with the same interest and commitment that we think about Europe or the US. And we need to move beyond some of the received wisdom and clichés that have contaminated our approach to China in the last half-century. We need to manoeuvre between the extremes of writing China off as a monolithic, inhumane one party state, and becoming new apologists for its failure to reform in key areas.

These days, it is more accurate to say that we are China collaborators. But what is this brave New China we are so assiduously creating? If we weren't that clear about what the old China was, which after all appears to have been many Chinas rolled into one, how can we be that clear about the new one? This book attempts to address some of the angles by which and through which we might see 'China' in order to be clearer about what to expect, and what to think in the years ahead, when China is an even greater presence in our lives than it is now.

I thought about many of the issues of this book in the rather different professions of a teacher (in Inner Mongolia, China, from 1994 to 1996, under the noble auspices of VSO (Voluntary Service Overseas)), a business person (working for a small company, now no longer in existence, in Kent from 1996 to 1998) and then as a diplomat at the Foreign and Commonwealth Office, in London and then Beijing, from 1998 to 2004. In that time, I managed to visit, for various purposes, and under various conditions and guises, all of China's 31 provinces, autonomous regions and municipalities. I travelled by plane, boat, car, bike, foot and, just once, horse, across various parts of China's enormous, varied territory, talking to people in some of the remotest regions (usually battling against impenetrable accents, rather than any cultural differences) and in the large, bursting cities. About most of the issues here, I have changed my mind if not once, then at least three or four times. This book, however, is the result of returning to full time engagement with China, both as an Associate Fellow at Chatham House, and as Director of a company helping to bring the Chinese private sector to the UK, Strategic China Ltd.

In the course of this lengthening, and sometimes intense engagement, I have appreciated the help of many people, only a few of whom I can mention here. Andrew Beale was, whether he likes it or not, my first teacher of Chinese, while I stayed in Melbourne, Australia in the early 1990s. His mastery of Mandarin was a great inspiration to me, as was his extensive knowledge of the recent history, and regions of China. I studied Chinese in the now sadly defunct one-year course, at Thames Valley University, London. However, the real work of learning Chinese was done in Hohhot, Inner Mongolia, and I am very grateful to my excellent teacher of Chinese there, and to other friends and students who helped me climb the mountain that I feel I have climbed only a few metres today. I am only too sorry that none of them were ever able to help me conquer the greatest challenge – Chinese tones.

I am grateful to Professor Flemming Christiansen for taking me on as a high-risk part-time PhD student at Leeds, in the late 1990s, and then steering me through two major life changes, when I almost abandoned my thesis. Like most, I reached the finishing line exhausted. The process of a

PhD was an enriching one, and without that behind me, I wouldn't have dared embark on a full-scale book like the one now. I am grateful, too, to those I got to know over the years working in the FCO (Foreign and Commonwealth Office) – Jasper Becker, who gave really excellent advice, as ever, when I showed him the first synopsis of this book; John Gittings, who read parts of it, and made some very useful comments; Nigel Cox, who was the first to trawl through the whole piece and give feedback, drawn from his long career as a diplomat working in China; Catherine Brown, who picked me up on some critical points; Jim O'Donoghue, who was ever encouraging and generous in his responses. I would also like to thank Christopher Segar, my mother Jacqueline Howe, Peter Brennan, Mobo Gao, Matthew Fletcher and Natalia Lissenkova for reading through the manuscript and offering comments and corrections. Needless to say (though it always needs saying) all the mistakes and errors left are entirely mine.

CHAPTER ONE:
CHINA AND THE TWO PATHS

Politicians and leaders in China, like everywhere else, have always liked metaphors. The treacherous political environment encouraged this. Speaking with metaphors avoided the pitfalls involved in baldly stating something and then being held to account for it. Metaphors supplied the insurance policy of ambiguity. At the dawn of the CR in 1966, the killer blow inflicted on the Vice Mayor of Beijing, Wu Han, after he had written a play about a clean Ming dynasty official hounded from office, was to have Mao Zedong bluntly state that the whole thing was an allegory about himself and his dismissal of one of his main Generals, Peng Dehuai, after criticizing him. From that point, Wu Han was walking wounded. He was among the CR's earliest high-level victims.

One of the most popular metaphors from the CR period was the one about the two paths. It had provenance long before this time, but sheer insistent usage got it irrevocably tied to that period. There was the good path, the path of the proletariat and the workers and the glorious Communist Party. And there was the bad path of the capitalists, colonialists, and landlords. Those who walked the capitalist path were simply written off as Capitalist Roaders. The two paths wound their separate ways, one to Utopia, and the other to oblivion. But three decades later, it seems they both have reached the same point – a Capitalist Socialist Utopian carnival.

Polarity, as I will argue later, is imbedded in modern Chinese discourse. The two paths are the staple means to convey this. So, it isn't inappropriate to use this metaphor now to set out the two sorts of future that China might have. Of course, as a recent book by one of the veterans of the 4 June Incident/Massacre, Wang Chaohua, put it, while there might be 'One China' (and we will look at this in more detail in the next chapter) there are in fact 'Many Paths'.[1] But for simplicity's sake, I'll draw out two extremes.

---

1   Wang Chaohua (ed), *One China, Many Paths*, London 2003.

And then spend the rest of the book working out which one is closest to what is likely.

Path One: Stable China

Fast-forward 20 years. It is now 2026. China overtook the US as the world's largest economy nearly a year previously, going faster than even the most bullish analysts had predicted a generation before. Chinese companies like Haier and Wa Haha, are among the best known global brands. China leads the world in the production of hi-tech equipment, and is a world leader in research and development. Through heavy government interventions, the wealth from the coastal areas has now reached deep into the hinterland. Some of the country's richest millionaires are in Xinjiang and Tibet. Even these remote cities have a thriving middle class with sophisticated consumer tastes and expectations. This process has effectively solved the historical issue of separatism by enfranchising most people in the border areas, making them realize they have more to lose than gain from secession with China. It has also meant that the central government has been able to grant more genuine autonomy to these regions, especially after the death of the potent symbolic figure of the Dalai Lama, and his replacement by a highly controversial Beijing-appointee.

Because of aggressive implementation of environmentally friendly policies in the 2000s and 2010s, people can now joke about the period of the great fog years before, when cities existed in a cloud of pollution. The massive process of urbanization is over. The division between the cities and the countryside has stabilized, and the living environment, after a glut of construction and building, is greatly improved. Cities are full of green spaces, and the car ownership problem has been partly solved by the use of a far higher proportion of liquid gas vehicles than in the West. China has built excellent public transport facilities in most of its cities, and vastly improved its flight network. Foreigners with memories of trying to get around the country in the dark ages of the 1980s and 1990s are laughed at when they say how tough it was back then. China also offers one of the best connected motorway and hi-speed train networks in the world.

In 2026, seven of the world's top banks are Chinese. Chinese companies make up over 50 per cent of the world's top companies. The Fortune 100 list consists of about 40 individuals who are based in China, or from China originally. The world's richest man is a 70-year old entrepreneur who made his money originally by devising the Chinese equivalent of Google, which then expanded into the provision of key financial services, taking the whole of the Chinese speaking world market. China is exporting its own technology abroad, though it is increasingly irritated at the IPR (Intellectual Property Rights) infringements occurring in the West and America, which it puts down to the desperation from their poor performing economies and high levels of unemployment. In 2025, China became the world's largest aid donor, and the largest outward investor, its colossal foreign reserves used to buy companies in Africa, Europe and America.

Business people visiting China are all expected to speak Chinese, as it has become the international language of trade. In most schools in Europe and the US, Chinese has become the most popular second language to study. The French government complained recently about the large number of Chinese loan words creeping into the French language. Things like 'La guangxi' for connections, and 'Le Gaoji Lingdao' for top-level leader. But, the French government, like most others, is wary of upsetting the Chinese, not only because of the vast amounts of investment being made into their country, but also because of the endless numbers of Chinese tourists filling their cities, and the huge revenues still being brought in by the second and third generation of Chinese students who have followed their parents abroad to study. Some laugh at the idea that in fact Europe serves three functions – as a school and university to the Chinese, as a tourist playground and as a source of cheap labour. Especially in Eastern Europe (which now embraces Russia), and the outer edges of the continent, many Chinese companies are setting up plants to manufacture their products for the market back home.

Pundits have been proved wrong by the constant predictions of the fall of the Communist Party. After some nasty hiccoughs in the 2010s, when three large demonstrations that nearly overthrew the Party were put down, the Party seems as strong as ever. It is a Marxist Capitalist orientated People's Party, with multi-class appeal, and with a thriving entrepreneurial cadre, who have been labelled the vanguard of the business revolutionaries. So successful has the Party been that it is now as closely studied and copied as the Japanese were at the peak of their powers almost half a century earlier. But people say there is a difference. The Chinese have patience and staying power. They will not drop away like the Japanese did. The first woman President of the US, Chelsea Clinton, declared during a recent Democratic Convention that the US needed to study the CPC (Chinese Communist Party), look to how it had maintained stability, and strengthened its economy. US officials have been sent on courses to the CPC School, looking to learn from them about new skills like opaque, and deep opaque management. There is also a huge amount of exchange between the People's Liberation Army (PLA) and the US Army, and both cooperated fully in the recent invasion of Russia, though the aftermath of this has proved difficult, with a UN peacekeeping force saying the country is sliding towards civil war and that the interim administration cannot cope, raising the spectre of the disastrous invasion of Iraq and the lengthy civil war that ensued two decades before.

With the shift in allegiance from Taiwan to China by the last country to recognize the government in Taipei, the leadership in the Republic of China are preparing for the fourth plebiscite on whether to enter talks for a final resolution to the problem of Taiwan's status. Popular opinion in Taiwan is now committed to the idea that unification is better than the current status of being independent but increasingly marginalized. There is even a strand of thought in China that believes the island is more of a burden than a gain, and shouldn't be accepted back. As the biggest giver of aid, with the largest military budget, China dominates Asia. It has secured compensation and apologies from Japan over the war almost a century before. Indonesia is indeed so reliant on Chinese aid that it recently allowed China to buy its three largest banks. The Prime Minister of Australia, himself ethnically Chinese, said that as Australia was now so much part of Asia, Australia had no objection.

It is internationally agreed that democracy, which was the most successful form of government in the last century, had severe limitations, and that the CPC has devised a new form, one party democracy, otherwise known as Intra-Party Democracy. Scholars and academics agree that democracy can successfully exist within a single party, if that party has diverse constituents and membership. This idea has been embraced internationally. Commentators have also agreed that the extreme low level of participation in western elections indicated a lack of interest and apathy, and a desire to return to older style authoritarianism. The governments of Austria and Italy have been at the forefront of introducing elections simply for important issues, via network portal points, and having governments run along the same lines as a company, with a board of directors elected by a panel, themselves chosen by institutions contracted to headhunt the best qualified leadership candidates.

As a result of these changes, the CPC has removed the controversial commitment to democracy previously slated to be implemented in 2050, contained in some of its official pronouncements. Its greatest challenge is simply how to deal with the recently unified Korea, which, having undergone over half a decade of streamlining, is looking set to become one of the world's greatest economic powerhouses, led by the dynamic leadership of Kim Jong Il's daughter. Part of the final deal was to allow the

South Koreans to maintain their political system for two decades, but to the surprise of everyone, the South Koreans are keen to embrace the hard line ideology of the north, which, having survived every attack, is now widely seen as far more resilient and robust than the weaker democratic models available.

Path Two: An Unstable China

In 2026, the pundits are united about one thing. The development of China that started over half a century before was, though, no one knew it at the time, effectively a death knell for the world's environment. Energy and natural resources had been totally overestimated and with no urgent research into alternative sources, what had happened was too little too late. China had simply, in its gallop towards a developed nation status, gulped up most of what the world had in two dazzling decades, in which it had posted official growth statistics of over 10 per cent each year. Having effectively exhausted the world's petrol and gas resources, it had built, with little real planning, a dozen massive nuclear power stations, one of which had had a disastrous accident in 2020, making over a third of Xinjiang in the north-west uninhabitable. The huge number of fatalities there had been seen, by many outside and inside the region, as a deliberate attempt to eradicate so-called separatist threat from the Muslims living there. This had only served to make the region even more unstable, with an increasingly active terrorist group now more than capable of making attacks deep within China. They had recently succeeded in assassinating a Vice Premier while on a visit to Shanghai.

China's handling of its ethnic minority regions was the least of its problems. The rapid expansion of the Chinese middle class had pushed car usage through the roof, shooting up from only 1 per cent to almost 25 per cent of the population owning cars. The roads in cities were in a state of permanent gridlock. 400 million cars were spouting out fumes that were simply choking the people to death. The joke that instead of a one child policy like in the old days, China would need a one car policy was no longer so funny. China looked like the first culture in the history of the world likely to simply be destroyed by the car.

The Chinese state is on its last legs. The strategy to have wealth trickle from the coastal regions inland stalled in the 2010s when it was realized that the capital investment in these areas, and the massive brain drain of human capital out of them, meant the task was far greater than had originally been predicted. Many cities, regions on the coast and richer areas reached crisis point in the mid 2010s, simply banning outsiders from coming in. This created a scenario similar to a city state, with increasingly strident appeals to local interests over national ones. Attempts to broker quotas for cities to accept outsiders broke down because of the amount of fraud and false documents being used. Foreign countries too, tired of this constant wave of people coming out of China, imposed increasingly restrictive requirements, including massive bonds, and even, in some countries (including the UK) electronic tags on Chinese nationals coming in which were only removed when they physically got on the plane or vessel out of the country. The UK had managed to introduce this measure despite strenuous opposition by both the European Union (EU) and the International Court of Human Rights, successfully arguing that the human rights of those in the UK were being violated by the hundreds of thousands of Chinese who had come into the country, only to sink underground and never leave. The sheer size of these communities had made them conspicuous and a major political problem for the government, which felt it had been forced into taking this measure.

The Central Government, in a nutshell, was simply incapable of running China. In many areas of the country regional governments and strongmen acted as they pleased. Some analysts predicted that by 2050, the country would no longer exist as a single entity. Sichuan, Yunan, and Guangzhou had already made clear signs of their desire to break away. Massive demonstrations in these areas had occurred throughout the last decade, with a weaker and weaker response by the PLA and the Central government each time. There were respected voices in Beijing that argued that, in many ways, with all it current problems, China was better off letting these restive and time consuming areas break away.

While there was no dispute about there being some rich people in China, there was great controversy about how many. A property boom in the 2010s had collapsed, along with a disastrous fall on the stock market, and the final convertibility of the Chinese Yuan, which had exposed it to speculative runs. All of this had seen many of the new middle class reduced to where they had started from two decades earlier. The fabled Chinese private sector had, in fact, been exposed as the state trying to pretend that some of its operations were in others' hands, even when they weren't. A string of high profile 'private companies' had collapsed, leaving massive debts, and causing hundreds of thousands to be laid off, creating the joke that this was the second 'falling into the pond' after the first in the 1990s. But this pond had proved itself to be far deeper than the one before. Increasing discontent had seen vicious uprisings in the 2010s, and in 2025, the latter by way and far the worst, with the PLA being unable to control over a million and a half protesters in Beijing who had torn down the walls of the central government compound with impunity. The full leadership of the party had been forced to resign, for the first time ever, and a new generation of leaders, mostly foreign educated, had taken their place. But these too had run out of ideas about how to deal with China's three great demons – instability, the environment and the poor.

Political scientists and economists now agreed that China never had been a state as such. It had operated as an informal coalition of interests, somehow producing the networks to keep the whole untidy unwieldy mess of what was called China together. But in fact, even in terms of the economy, there had been an elite who had stockpiled enormous wealth, squirreling massive amounts of it abroad, and meaning that both the banks, and companies, and indeed all of the construction and economic activity in China were built on thin air. The great dreams of the twenty-first century belonging to China were now regarded as nothing more than a bad joke. Statisticians and researchers had long since given up believing any of the statistics produced from the 1980s. China's growth rate, it was now agreed, was far lower than any of these had ever stated. Its economic growth was called the greatest myth after Atlantis and the Bermuda Triangle.

Because of its geopolitical importance, however, foreign countries had been impelled to sink increasing amounts of money into the country, through the World Bank (WB) and International Monetary Fund (IMF). The latest injection of 3 trillion dollars in 2024 had barely managed to scratch the surface. Far from there being black holes deep in space, people joked, there was one stretching from Urumqi to Beijing. China was largely off-limits for tourists and visitors because of the instability, and the lack of faith in the government being able to deliver basic levels of safety. All of this was topped by the unruliness of the PLA, underfunded and now deeply resentful, which had threatened at several times to stage a military coup. The PLA had funded its activities through massive, unscrupulous sales of arms to third countries, and within China. There were clear signs of well-resourced local militia growing up in central and southern China. Hong Kong had long since become the fiefdom of the Guangzhou Group, as they had called it, who had effectively milked the special region dry, and made it nothing more than the centre for their smuggling, gambling and prostitution rackets. Macao had proved far too small for their ambitions and had simply been made into a Chinese style Disneyland location.

There was increasing talk among those in touch with the Chinese on the Mainland of a yearning to return to the good old days, especially the golden

age, running from the 1960s to the 1970s, when China was stable and safe.
Those old enough to remember reminisced about the simplicity of life then.
Mao Zedong had made an extraordinary comeback, celebrated by people as
a strong, honest ruler who had managed to keep the country clean, and stop
the cancers of corruption and nepotism that had since spread through the
Chinese body politic. There was good evidence that a modern form of
slavery had been reinvented, with credible accounts of people in markets in
the main urban centres and one outrageous story of a human safari park in
Guangzhou where wealthy 'hunters' went in search of humans, killing and
then eating them. This was taken as a symbol of the general nihilism most
Chinese suffered, with massive institutions set up and chaotically run simply
to look after those who had, in effect, lost their minds. The Chinese looked
enviously at the Russians who, after decades of hardship, had created one of
the world's most dynamic economies, had just overtaken the US, and were
fast catching up on the newly unified Federal European State (FES), created
by the Treat of London in 2024, as the world's largest economy.

Which One?

In fact, even those with a superficial knowledge of China will recognize
themes in both the stable and unstable paths above that could be said to be
true now. China is wracked with problems due to its lack of transparency,
environmental degradation, instability – all of this being dealt with by an
authoritarian governmental system simply not used to listening to certain
kinds of opinions. China's transitional phase seems never-ending. Will it
break up? Will it go from strength to strength, supplanting the US some
time later this century, as the world's premier superpower? Are all our
current fears empty worries, or should we really be concerned that a country
that, on the surface at least, presents such different approaches to human
rights, economic and business conduct, and international diplomacy, is likely
to become increasingly important?

In any one week now, there are myriad articles in the press, programmes
on TV, lectures and talks in universities and to societies, about the Coming
Rise of China. This month alone (February 2006) while the Three Dynasties
exhibition reaches its end, after a decent turnout at the Royal Academy, the
Chinese New Year of the Dog is celebrated by the Mayor of London in the
underground with posters and even Chinese poems in characters beside
English translations. Channel Four and the Guardian run features on
Chongqing, 'the world's largest city that no one has ever heard of', a fertilizer
manufacturer from Xian (one of China's few women entrepreneurs) raises 94

million pounds for her company by listing on the Alternative Investment Market in London, and the US Congress restates its demands that the Chinese revalue the Chinese Yuan after posting yet more record export figures. This is all crowned by the statement that China has overtaken Japan as the largest holder of foreign exchange in the world (863 billion USD as opposed to 860 billion USD). 84 thousand Chinese students still come to the UK, despite the prohibitive exchange rates making the costs of their studies far higher. An academic at the London School of Economics (LSE) tells me that they alone receive 3000 applications from the Chinese every month. Another eminent academic in Cambridge remarks that the university is so full of BMW driving wealthy Chinese students they almost merit an anthropological study in their own right.

From being a place three decades ago encapsulated by the metaphor of the bamboo curtain, glimpsed at sporadically, mysterious and remote, China is all around us, its goods in our shops and supermarkets. Tescos and Wal-Mart source huge quantities of their merchandise from China – a country they are now both opening their own stores in to cap the swelling middle class consumer market there. China is gobbling up our energy resources (biggest user of all energy apart from oil, where it runs the US a distant but rapidly closing in second), one of the world's biggest polluters (seven of the world's ten most polluted cities are in China), and an endless source of migrants, who join an overseas Chinese population with formidable economic resources. China is buying up our companies (IBM, now Lenovo in the US, and MG Rover, now owned by Nanjing Auto in the UK). Its tourists are flooding into our cities (placed, in the UK at least, on an Approved Tourist Destination list in 2005, meaning that visas are now theoretically easier to get), its language is being taught in our schools (Brighton College erroneously claimed it was the first to offer this last year, but in fact many other schools now offer Mandarin to all students).

Now is as good a time as ever to work out what sort of China we would like to see in 20 years time. We might well feel nostalgic for the past when China remained enclosed within its own barriers. One of the recurring themes of this book is the long tradition of wishful thinking on both sides of the divide – Chinese and outsider – after, of course, this divide has been located. The strong assertions of 'Chinese unity' and homogeneity are one of the perplexing issues looked at in the next chapter. But in fact, there are good, well proved traditions of outsiders significantly changing the entity that was, and has become, China – positively and negatively, from the reviled Opium Wars of a century ago, to the importation of new thinking and ideologies by figures as diverse as Bertrand Russell and John Dewey in the early twentieth century that inspired the initial reforms of the Republican Chinese period. The China that exists now, in fact, can be seen as an amazing hybrid of external and internal forces, combining *Chinese* Marxist-Leninism (the italics are important), *Chinese* socialism, and all out, raw capitalism – all within the *Chinese* centralized state. Each of these areas combines clearly externally sourced impetuses with internal issues to create wholly new entities. Perhaps as the twenty-first century carries on, we can engage and participate in the evolution of this entity, which despite its rhetoric and strong assertions of unity and integrity, is in fact far more open to influence than we might at first think. In that sense, the choice between a, stable or unstable China or any version in between, becomes as much ours as those in China. But before we think about which China we want, we had better be clear about what China we are looking at. That is the subject of the next chapter.

CHAPTER TWO:
WHAT DO WE MEAN WHEN WE
SAY CHINA?

We read, speak, hear daily about China, and take it as a given. But the current term, 'China' is, in the jargon of discourse analysts, highly contested. The China of 1947 was not the same as the China of 1997, or of 1897. It has evolved, developed and changed radically over the last few hundred years. That complicated, multi-layered history has contributed to the myriad paradoxes that China now contains. It also means that people with widely different perspectives can still talk validly about 'China' simply because there is no single settled thing it might be said they are talking about.

Questioning the concept 'China' is not just a diverting postmodernist game. Julia Lovell, in her recent book about the various myths of 'The Great Wall' writes about the fact that two centuries ago, 'China', the two characters for 'middle country' didn't actually exist as a term.[1] Dynasties referred to themselves simply by their name – Tang, Song, Ming, Qing. The dynasties *were* the countries. And as I will elaborate a little later, the countries they referred to became radically different from each other over time.

The greatest political achievement of Mao Zedong, granted by most of even his most virulent detractors (with the exception of Jung Chang and Jon Halliday's recent onslaught on the Chairman in *Mao: The Unknown Story*) was to create a unified country. This country, I will call, for the sake of convenience, the PRC. It is different from those Chinas that preceded it. Over the centuries, entities that existed before have been divided up, split and diffracted. In the century before the PRC's foundation, 'China' was for long periods subject to foreign influence, or to the whims of regional warlords, and then finally split evenly between the territory under the control of the nationalists under Chang Kaishek, and the Communists,

---

1   *The Great Wall: China Against the World, 1000 BC–2000 AD,* London, 2006.

under Mao. 1949, seemingly, marked the moment when these divisions were repaired. A unified People's Republic could, indeed, stand up, and face the rest of the world, restored to its original united glory.

The Story of the Regions

But it wasn't quite as straightforward as that. Firstly, there was unfinished business in extending the limits of the 1949 state over border territories. Inner Mongolia, for instance, offers a case in point. Mao had promised the Mongolians, in a famous speech in 1935, that with a Communist victory they would be granted independence.[2] They had, after all, been a semi-independent zone, under the control of the Japanese from 1932. Prior to that there had been active moves in the 1920s and 1930s to come closer to the Mongolian People's Republic, founded in 1921. In their earliest interactions with the Chinese communists, the Inner Mongolian representatives spoke as equals, and certainly aspired to being something more than a region of the future greater Chinese state. But their reward, at least initially in 1949, was to be offered 'autonomous region' status – a status the special powers of which were to be progressively whittled down as the years passed. This process was greatly facilitated by the influx of ethnically Han settlers into the area over the years, meaning that, by the 1980s, only 10 per cent of the local population of Inner Mongolia could actually claim that they were Mongolian. Intermarriage watered this down even further.

The north-western province of Xinjiang followed a similar pattern. Only here, an independent state, the Peoples Republic of Turkmenistan, actually existed from 1945 to 1949. Rich in natural resources, and comprising 16 per cent of the whole of the Chinese landmass, Xinjiang has tenuous cultural and social links with other Chinese regions. It was inhabited predominantly by Muslims (even today, about 50 per cent of the population are still Muslims). Its culture, architecture, and social practices were closer to the other 'Stan' countries, previously in the former USSR, rather than Asia. Offered the same 'autonomous region' status as Inner Mongolia, it was to embrace this with fractiousness and dissent, which continues into the twenty-first century. The Central government has consistently tried to place Muslim groups agitating for independence from China on the list of terrorist organizations recognized by the US after the 11 September, 2001 attacks.

---

2   Quoted in Stuart Schram (ed), *Mao's Road to Power: Revolutionary Writings 1912–1949, Volume Five: Towards the Second United Front*, London, 1999, 71.

They have blamed these groups for bomb attacks in Beijing and other Chinese cities. As with Inner Mongolia, a concerted effort to settle more Han into the region has diluted its ethnic composition. But to any visitor, it remains a part of China with a very different feel.

And finally Tibet, not even part of the PRC on its foundation in 1949, but 'acquired' between 1951 and 1959, through a series of 'agreements' and 'pacts'. Tibet has remained the most resolutely and stubbornly 'other' of the PRC territory – a place that, because of lack of access and sheer geographical inhospitality, was less easy to tie to the rest of China. Even long term Han residents tended to serve their time there, then return to their original home. China's historical claims on Tibet are complicated. The position, even now, of at least the British government is to recognize 'suzerainty' (special influence) of China in the region, but not sovereignty – perhaps as good an illustration as any of the controversy that Tibet's participation in the contemporary Chinese state still arouses.

The Problem of Chinese Unity

All of this is, ostensibly, not surprising. The US, as a sovereign nation, contains huge ethnic diversity. Russia and Turkey, as two more obvious examples, contain significant territories where people have good arguments for their autonomy and separate identity. But for China, one of the key claims in the last half-century of unity, is that such unity is an indispensable part of being Chinese, and that it is based on a shared history of 5,000 years of continuous civilization and culture[3]. Thus the anxiety to extend clear cultural and historical links to other ethnic groups within its current borders. This is where things get difficult.

The idea of Chinese homogeneity and unity was compounded by the years of Maoist enclosure. At the peak of the CR in the late 1960s, China had only one ambassador based abroad. Foreign experience and interaction with China, if not through refugees or those who had emigrated out much

---

3   An experienced UK-based commentator on China wryly noted, when I mentioned the curious case of the `5000 years of continuous Chinese culture' so often spoken of in China, that this figure seemed to suffer from its own specific inflationary pressure. For many years, it seems, people had talked about three or four thousand years of history, until former President Jiang Zemin visited Egypt in the late 1990s. It seemed the encounter with one of the few countries in the world with a competing claim to immense antiquity and continuity made the addition of an extra 1000 years an urgent necessity.

earlier, was very limited. The few images and stories that filtered out of the mysterious red bamboo kingdom then revealed a country of grinding uniformity. People dressed the same, looked the same, and seemed to be thinking the same thoughts in the same language. From the northern deserts bordering Mongolia to the southern island of Hainan, China in those early decades of the PRC did look like a mighty united army.

Can history help us in working out what is behind these strong claims to unity? Surely, if the idea is simply that there has been a continuous civilization for over five millennia, then there must be a distinct geographical location for this great uniform civilization. But a traveller in the modern geographical entity of the PRC has a choice of former capitals to choose from; Xian, the reigning Chinese city during the Tang and Song dynasties, or even Taiyuan, which was the capital further back. Maybe Chongqing, brief holder of the prize under the rule of Chang Kaishek, or Beijing, on and off capital since it was designated as the Summer City during the rule of the Khans almost a millennium ago. The more imaginative could even turn their eyes to Yuan Shang Du in the Inner Mongolian grasslands, now deserted, but once the Yuan Dynasty's winter capital, a memory, an inspiration for Xanadu and immortalized in Marco Polo's visit there eight centuries ago (a visit, according to Sinologist Frances Wood, he may never have made).[4]

Students can dig deeper. They can look at maps of the various territories, borders and empires that China has encompassed over the centuries. Rather like splitting up a worm and watching the various segments wriggle apart into separate life forms, they can observe the periods when there were not one or two, or even three Chinas, but as many as five – during the Warring States period, or the Five Kingdoms. Perhaps at this point, they can wonder whether China does not, in some ways, more resemble a lose confederation like Europe, an assembly of viable smaller national states drawn together by political expediency and force. And they can also ponder the words that kick off the popular Chinese classic, *Romance of the Three Kingdoms* by Luo Guanzhong: 'The world under heaven, after a long period of division, tends to unite; after a long period of union, tends to divide. This has been so since antiquity.'[5]

---

4   Frances Wood, *Did Marco Polo Go To China?*, London 1995.
5   Translation from http://www.threekingdoms.com/chapter.php?c=1, accessed 16 May 2006.

Modern China, the PRC, is better viewed as an empire. It is an entity that straddles disparate cultures, unifying them with a political system, and solidifying this with certain standards of cultural and social interaction. This colonization has been greatly helped by three things. The first is the immense unifying power of the Chinese written language, compounded in the last half-century by the spread of Mandarin throughout China (a force, it should be stressed, as potent in its ability to unify as that of the use of the Roman alphabet in most of contemporary Europe). The second is the drive by the PRC central government to link all parts of the great empire into one whole through trains, air links and roads. And the final force is the general desire of the ruling Communist Party to see a stable China, and that means unity.

Such an empire has claims upon areas beyond its reach. The Spratly Islands, for instance, parts of the South China Sea and islands that at the moment ostensibly belong to Japan. And of course, the trickiest of all, the Republic of Taiwan, a sovereign state in all but name, and dealt with, over the last few decades since it broke from China, as part of One China, with no one currently saying which part belongs to whom.

William Van Kemenade called this phenomenon of multiple Chinas something akin to China Inc., a massive holding company with a number of subsidiaries beneath it.[6] But the current China has been an enormous and costly enterprise to create – and carries some deep and worrying fault lines. The main ones can be divided across ethnic and social lines. And both are not so easily resolved, no matter how much one listens to the rhetoric of the central government about China being unified and one.

Ethnicity and its Problems

Ethnicity, or what the PRC calls it's national minorities, is not just an issue in the three border areas mentioned above that contain high numbers of non-Han people. The PRC currently has 55 recognized ethnic minorities, spread throughout the county, making up 7 per cent of its population. Researchers have shown that this figure was reached fairly arbitrarily. Areas with potentially dozens or even hundreds of ethnic minorities like Sichuan

---

6   William van Kemenade, *China, Hong Kong, Taiwan, Inc: The Dynamics of a New Empire*, New York 1998.

were in fact, during the construction of this list, allocated a specific number. 55 was decided before the fieldworkers even knew what they would find.[7]

Of these 55 minorities, the PRC guaranteed equality before the law in its earliest constitution in the 1950s. But there was always a very real sense that while some forms of ethnic self-expression were permissible, others were not – and the boundary between these, like the boundaries of the PRC, were always shifting. Dancing, wearing 'ethnic costumes', eating ethnic food – all that kind of thing was allowed (except during the highly xenophobic period of the CR). But any straying towards expressions of identity that were seen as demanding autonomy, threatening the idea of the PRC's unity, stepping on the toes of national alliance, were quickly curtailed.

In the more paranoid periods of the PRC's history (for which read any major campaign, or power struggle, local or national and the whole of the CR), it was easy to see how minorities were going to be one of the first groups to come under renewed suspicion. The key question then was quite simply were you for or against the vision of a strong, unified state that Mao Zedong's government had set up. This may have been framed in questions about ideology, but that, in the end, simply harked back to a demand to know whose side you were on. Mao put this very bluntly in his first published essay, 'Who are our enemies? Who are our friends? That is the key question of Revolution'.[8] All too often, as so frequently with minority groups, they could be fingered very early on as people whose difference betrayed questionable allegiance.

To be Mongolian or Muslim in China is to be a minority – a minority with minority rights, and a specific ideology of nationality to support this. As one Uiguar I met in Xinjiang put this to me a decade ago, 'Why is it that in my own home, my own territory, surrounded by my own people, I am still labelled a minority? Does that mean that for the whole of my life I am beholden to a majority, and must always surrender to them?' Being Chinese, but also ethnically non-Han, means fighting two wars – one to maintain your identity with the tools that are allowed you, and the other is to work out how far you are even going to be allowed to be what you are.

---

7   For more on this, see Thomas S Mullaney, '55+1=55 or the Strange Calculus of Chinese Nationhood' in *China Information* Vol XVIII, No 11, July 2004.
8   Mao Zedong, 'Analysis of the Classes in Chinese Society', March 1926, in Mao Zedong, *Selected Works*, Volume I, Beijing 1963, 13.

Social Unity

Social fault lines are a tougher call. For business people, it has become a cliché now to say that in fact, the PRC is not one market, but at the very least three. There are the top 100 million, who are the real winners of the reform process over the last three decades. There are the second level wealthy and the 200 million who are doing OK, but have aspirations for something better. Then there are the vast numbers of the rural and urban poor – people who in some areas earn far less than the UN designated one dollar a day to qualify for absolute poverty.

This stratification of PRC society will be a recurrent theme in this book. From the word go, the issue of how to classify different strata in PRC society was a serious one. For Mao Zedong, it became the absolute 'life or death' article of his new ideology. Even while stressing the need for unity, and for the creation of a new national consensus, he was also creating the divide between the 'Old China', feudal, repressive, riven by class conflict, and the 'New China', led by the workers and proletariat, though in fact this turned out to be more the rural population, who were the ones who most supported his great revolutionary drive.

These days, these classifications can be mapped geographically. The Eastern region of China, the great outward looking coastal provinces like Fujian and Shandong, have developed rapidly since 1980. They contain some of the wealthiest, newest cities (crowned by Shanghai), and are areas of immense industrial growth and energy. Then there are the inland provinces, places like Hunan, Anhui and Henan. These have lagged behind, though because of transport links, and more plentiful and cheaper labour over the last decade, they have started catching up. Their cities are now smothered with the same skyscrapers and the Western brand displays as coastal ones. Behind these, stretches the huge undeveloped western region, containing places like Tibet, Shaanxi, Gansu. These are more sparsely populated, less interlinked to the rest of China, with large areas of severe poverty. The western region has been the focus of a central government campaign since 2000 to develop and open it up, seeing in some places rich coastal provinces 'adopt' sister provinces inland and channel investment towards them. Those who do business in these regions often say that it presents the same challenges as the first areas to open up in China almost 30 years ago.

The critical point to notice is that all of these ethnically, socially and geographically diverse areas are asserted by the central government to be part of a unified, one Party state. And unity has been one of the non-negotiables of political discourse for the last 60 years. Unity was what was asserted up to and during 1949 and the creation of the PRC. It was the guiding inspiration behind the earliest, optimistic political campaigns in the 1950s. In the chaos of the CR, although it may not have looked and felt like it, unity was uppermost in everyone's minds, and flogged to death in the propaganda then. After Mao's death, whatever the changes, unity was what was standing behind them, deep into the 1980s, after the fall of the Berlin Wall and the break up of Eastern Europe, Deng Xiaoping's government simply asserted unity as their excuse to send the tanks in on 4 June 1989. The 'third' and 'fourth' generation of leaders after him, Jiang Zemin and Hu Jintao, all asserted that maintaining unity was their top priority. Unity crops up everywhere. A highly urbane and intelligent academic from Zhejiang province told me at a conference there in 2004 that the practice of discourse analysis, while perfectly OK to point at Chinese language texts, needed to be always inspired and motivated by 'the need to preserve unity'. He seemed unaware of the irony of his firmly asserting one area of discourse being unavailable to the same rigorous analysis and deconstruction as others.

The Side Effects of Unity

Once 'unity' gets in through the door, a whole legion of other assumptions and stereotypes follow behind to back it up. Take, for instance the puzzling statement that China is the world's 'oldest longest continuous civilization' with 'five thousand years of history' – a statement that can be found in many guide books about China. It's hard to work out what this 'five thousand years' applies to. There is certainly no continuous territorial state that has that sort of longevity, nor for that matter, any specific group of people that could be said to be 5,000 years old. The 5,000 years of history spawns a host of connected myths – a unified 'Chinese food', unified 'Chinese character',and a shared 'Chinese sense of Confucian values'. All of these tend to fragment under analysis. What is, for instance, the characteristic of 'Chinese food'? A journey from the coast inwards, towards Inner Mongolia and Shanxi, will cross, on the olfactory map, fish, sea slug, abalone, then in Beijing the feted Beijing duck, and, in Shanxi, the local delicacy of pure pigs fat cooked in soya sauce (good, apparently, as a source of energy in the winter). In Inner Mongolia, it is mutton all the way. Deep down in Sichuan, there is excellent vegetarian food. There is nothing uniting any of these dishes, either in the way they are cooked, or what they are, apart from the simple fact that they are eaten in the entity we now call the PRC.

Outsiders seem to need this myth of unity and unified behaviour as much as those inside. Take this passage from a book about branding in China by an American:

Chinese, regardless of whether they live in China, Taiwan, or Hong Kong, are essentially the same. They are Confucian at the core. They share the same worldview based on a belief in fate, cyclical dynasticism, and go-with-the-flow Daoism. They have much in common in terms of broad social and business tendencies: filial piety (i.e.deference to authority figures, especially the father), comfort with/reliance on hierarchy; avoidance of the subjective; respect for mathematicians, disdain for humanities; round tables; strong personal ambition; a competitive worldview; reliance on fortune tellers and *feng shui*; intergenerational repression; commercial aggression; individualistic suppression; fear of uncertainty; low crime rates; investment in education... Hello Kitty stickers and kung fu flicks.[9]

Beyond the presumptive crassness of trying to bundle 1.3 billion people into such a 'pick and mix' hodgepodge, there lies the deadly fact that, over the years, similar lazy platitudes have been surrendered by ethnic Chinese from Hong Kong or other overseas communities, and including people like former Prime Minister of Singapore, Lee Kuan Yew, about 'Asian values' or 'Asian morality', giving this a sheen of credibility. Bringing analytic attention to these concepts usually results in them disappearing in a relativistic fog. But like rumours about Elvis Presley not being dead, or the Loch Ness Monster, they seem to have an amazing retentiveness, based more on emotional attachment than logic.

In 2006, to be Chinese in this unified way is extremely convenient. It means that what should be ungovernable becomes, by sleight of hand, just about governable, and the impossible mixtures of people, cultures and habits that exist in the PRC are held together far more strongly by believing in the myth of their own unity. But in order to achieve this, some highly paradoxical things need to be accommodated. The nature of these paradoxes, how they impact on what we do with China, and what China we might end up seeing, is explored in the following chapters.

Old myths die hard. In fact, they become almost part of another self-sustaining 'anti-reality'. The Great Wall, for instance, which in fact should be more truly called great walls, as there are several continuous different structures now so named, is still solemnly stated to be the only human structure visible from space. The first Chinese astronaut, a man called Yang, on his return to earth in 2004, had to admit that he had, in fact, not seen the

---

9   Tom Doctoroff, *Billions: Selling to the New Chinese Consumer*, New York 2005, pp. 107–8.

Great Wall when peering through his spaceship window. Nor indeed, has anyone else. But still the myth persists, perhaps because it is a nice myth. The myth of Chinese unity, while not so nice, is more necessary – for those inside the PRC, and for us grappling with it and what it means outside. But the cost of this is that, when talking about China, one is almost always allowed to contradict oneself, simply because it is never quite certain what one is talking about. And the fallout, as this book will often show, is that in talking about China, in the language of a unified China, one often feels like one is talking a second language over which one has imperfect command and in which now and then, the grammar and the vocabulary simply break down. But alas, there is no other language to talk in and be understood. That can be called the real achievement of the myth of Chinese unity – that it has made discourse about China impossible without accepting at least its terms, if not its content. As a slight sign of resistance to this, I will therefore, for the rest of this book, simply refer to the PRC, and no longer talk about China. The PRC is the entity we are dealing with today. Its fate is what interests us and will have an impact on us. 'China', which China, where, what type of China, is a subject that will simply need to be left here.

CHAPTER THREE:
A MAO FOR ALL SEASONS: THE MASTER
ON CONTRADICTIONS IN THE
TWENTY-FIRST CENTURY

Mao Zedong's shadow should be barely visible by now. According to the American historian of China, the late J K Fairbank, Mao's revolution was buried with him when he died in September 1976. But, as Belgian sinologist Simon Leys pointed out in the 1980s, Mao's influence is profound and far-reaching. On the day he died in September 1976, the streets of Beijing were full of weeping people. Despite the many attempts to bury or obliterate him in the years since, he remains an unsettling and disturbing presence. The outraged and defensive reaction in China to the all-out attack on Mao in Jung Chang and Jon Halliday's recent biography shows that his influence remains potent.[1] Mao may be a historical figure, but he will also figure in the PRC's future. This chapter explains why and how.

The Face of the Chairman

The only place where there are images of Mao these days, ironically, is either on the Tiananmen Square rostrum in the centre of Beijing (an image that was struck by paint bombs in the June 1989 events, an act that brought lengthy prison sentences to the protagonists) or on Chinese money. The appearance of Mao's image on money is an interesting recent development. Mao's face did appear on very early notes issued by the Communists in the areas they controlled in the 1930s. But almost as resistance to this sort of one-man worship, PRC money from 1949 onwards contained no images of specific personalities – just scenes of development (dams, bridges etc), or stereotyped images of the various ethnic minorities or social classes. That the

---

1   Jung Chang and Jon Halliday, *Mao: The Unknown Story*, London 2005.

PRC's final surrender to capitalism and market forces in all but name should be accompanied by the reappearance of its founder on the money that is so central to this new culture could almost be seen either as a grand gesture of irony, or an attempt to assuage guilt.

Part of the problem, as Helmut Martin alluded to in a study of Mao's works, is simply of being precise about which Mao one might be talking about.[2] Mao's character maps out the contradictions and paradoxes of the place he did so much to bring into being and guide. The 'private' Mao, recorded in his personal doctor, Li Zhisui's, account, was a reckless, egotistical sensualist – a man who literally believed that nature could be curbed to human will, and who regarded himself as the central player in a new, magnificent dynasty.[3] The public Mao, however, was a far more cautious, mysterious figure – someone who never actually spoke directly to his people through television or radio after 1949, who had only sporadic contact with the public until the great Red Guard rally outings of the CR in 1967 and who existed behind a carefully constructed screen of remoteness and infallibility. This Mao, as his various, ill-fated chosen successors were all to learn, had a bad habit of withdrawing from public life only to reappear again, causing havoc.

The two Maos are reflected in the works he published, which, ironically, were his main source of income during his time in power (he received only a nominal wage as Party Chairman). Unrehearsed Mao, as Stuart Schram has labelled him, littered his speeches to Party groups and visiting delegations with copious, earthy invective. Of General Peng Dehuai, one of the heroes of the struggle for liberation, and a man brave enough to criticize Mao's economic policies during the Great Leap Forward period in the 1950s, Mao's caustic comment was that 'Peng has been trying to fuck me for ten years'. In his speeches he was not averse to talking of bodily functions and of using heavy sexual innuendo.[4]

All of this was ironed out in the published versions of his works. The original 'Concerning the Ten Contradictions Amongst the People' issued in 1957, and regarded as one of Mao's key theoretical texts, was a rambling, ill organized speech, given to what must have been a bewildered, if sporadically amused group of Party members. The original can be found in

---

2   Helmut Martin, 'Cult and Canon, Origins and Development of State Maoism, 1935–1978, New York 1981.

3   Li Zhisui, The Private Life of Chairman Mao, New York 1996.

4   Stuart R Schram, Mao Tsetung Unrehearsed, Harmondsworth 1974.

The Secret Speeches of Chairman Mao issued in 1989. The 'canonical' version was heavily edited, the colloquialisms taken out, and the whole speech literally rewritten. A similar process occurred for almost all of Mao's other major speeches, which were turned by a team of writers (led by Chen Boda, Mao's chief propagandist, who was felled in the early 1970s, and spent most of the rest of his life in jail before his death in 1989) into palatable literary works worthy of the Mao brand.

In the CR, there was a sizeable industry in producing variant rebellious group versions of 'Mao's latest sayings' or Mao's highest instructions. Relating a thought back to the Chairman was one of the few ways of legitimizing it, though the issue of authenticity infests this material. How could one man, normally so remote and inaccessible, be able to talk to so many visiting groups? Mao's pronouncements became increasingly gnomic and impenetrable – something that was to happen to subsequent paramount leader, Deng Xiaoping later in his career. He issued one-sentence instructions, which were then unleashed on an eager and obedient public. A single approving gesture resulted in the massive 'Learn from Dazhai' movement, which held up the Shanxi province commune in northern China as the model for the rest of the country. The falsification and lies upon which this particular Mao-created myth was built has been ably documented by, among others Liang Heng and Judith Shapiro who visited the place in the 1980s and found that its production returns were, literally, impossible and that the great harvests it had claimed were all fabricated.[5]

Mao might disappear, but he has a habit of making comebacks. On the centenary of his birth in 1993, the BBC pulled general opprobrium down upon its head by screening a documentary about him that was highly critical and contained an interview with his personal doctor, Li Zhisui, mentioned above. Such openness was seen by many in China as a colossal loss of face. 'We all know about his lovers and his dissolute life style', one friend, a teacher in a university, told me in 1994, 'but we don't, as Chinese, like seeing it talked about so vulgarly by foreigners'. Her conflation of Mao's face, and the face of the Chinese, puts its finger on one of the reasons why Mao is still such a sensitive figure. Open attacks on Mao are attacks on the myths and narratives that sustain the modern PRC. The equation goes like this. Mao was the man who stood up against bullying foreigners, who ended the years of humiliation, who united China into the PRC and made it strong. Attacks on him are attacks on the entity, which he fathered and

---

5   Liang Heng and Judith Shapiro, *Son of the Revolution* New York 1983.

produced. All of this resists even quite sound historical issues about whether or not Mao collaborated with the Japanese, and how much he was under the influence of Stalin.[6] Mao touches on emotional issues that evade rational discussion. As Liu Tuo, a Chinese intellectual and editor of the magazine, *Today* pointed out, 'Mao's writing is very different from writing in general and has become a separate genre in itself'.[7]

There is a Mao for all seasons. In the mid 1990s after several quiet years, Mao made a comeback as a mythical figure, appearing in cheap trinkets and on signs hung from taxi rear- view windows and in peasant houses.[8] I was always astonished to see, even in the late 1990s, the iconic images of Mao carefully pinned on to the walls of yurts and huts in Inner Mongolia by people who I knew had suffered dreadfully under movements which were directly inspired by him. The fervent 'Mao Zedong was a great leader' which preceded every toast then has become less common now – but those that muck around with the Chairman's image, words, or reputation, are straying into dangerous territory – the zone, where one passes from the permissible into the outlawed, where the agents of repression have a habit of suddenly cropping up.

Mao as Paradox

The very fact that Mao is a paradoxical figure means that thinking about him is a useful way in understanding some of the other paradoxes that now constitute the PRC. The combination of artificiality, make-believe and sheer downright lies in what has gone into creating the image of Mao and reflects much on the place that has produced this mythos. Mao himself celebrated conflict, contradiction and tension. He famously opined that 'without destruction there can be no construction', an idea that was enshrined in the CR, and became the justification for many of the acts of violence then.

It is not surprising, therefore, that he attempted to give this celebration of antagonism and conflict an intellectual garnish. His essay, 'On Contradiction', written in 1937, is widely regarded as his most accomplished

---

6   This, in essence, is the argument of Jung Chang and John Haliday in their *Mao, the Untold Story*.

7   In Liu Kang, Xiaobang Tang Eds, *Politics, Ideology and Literary Discourse in Modern China* Durham and London 1993, p 274.

8   Geremie Barme has dealt with this phenomenon in detail in *Shades of Mao: The Posthumous Cult of the Great Leader*, New York 1995.

theoretical work. 'The law of contradictions in things, that is, the law of the unity of opposites, is the basic law of nature and society, and therefore also the basic law of thought', he declared. In this essay, Mao demonstrated his main talent — importing abstractions from the master communist ideology and adapting them to concrete situations in China. Contradictions became a keyword in Mao's political lexicon, one of the few that lasted the next four decades till his death. He described them meticulously in 'The Ten Great Relationships'. The acceptance of Mao's teachings on contradictions (and after all, when asked by American journalist Edgar Snow during his celebrated interviews with the Chairman in the 1960s, Mao said that he was first and foremost a teacher, leaving politics as a sideline) is exemplified by an editorial in the *People's Daily*, the official organ of the Party even to this day, which in April 1956 declared that 'society at all times develops through continuous contradictions'.

The practical impact of this celebration of constant contradictions was a society in a state of permanent revolution after 1949, shifting from one campaign to the next, with no resting place and with polarization institutionalized and embedded. Social classes, for instance, were one of the main means to describe, and then work through, contradictions. The good classes were set against the bad classes, with increasingly disastrous result. By the CR, contradictions in society had almost worked its way up to all-out civil war. Mao seemed to regard such discord as both inevitable, and positive. The bottom line of his philosophy was simply that you couldn't make omelettes without smashing eggs.

That Marx, or Engels would have endorsed such a literal interpretation of dialectic materialism is questionable. In their pleasingly synthesized accounts, thesis and antithesis worked themselves forward like the gentle ticking of an old clock. Mao was keener on a form of intellectual nuclear fusion, bringing polarities crashing together and then seeing what happened when the dust clouds cleared, and the pieces settled. For four decades, the PRC's national ideology was predicated on a basis of instability, insecurity, and conflict, the eggs broken to make this particular omelette the thousands of individuals who fell on the wrong side of the divide.

Quoting Mao's theories on Contradictions these days is the sure way to raise a wry smile on the faces of whatever Chinese interlocutor you happen to be speaking to. Most will be astonished that you even know of this arcane work. But, in fact, the impact of Mao's thinking here is not so easily abandoned. In his dazzling essay in Rem Koolhass's *The Great Leap Forward*, Mihai Craciun ponders on the vagaries of ideology in contemporary PRC, and the material manifestations of this in the layout of the increasingly urbanized Chinese landscape.[9]

In the unified modern PRC, united around a commitment to development and forward progress, there sits, at the apex, a single party declaring the utter paramount importance of socialism with market characteristics. This is usually abbreviated to market socialism. The phrase is used so often now, as to appear almost unquestionable. But in fact, it is the greatest paradox of all. Socialism and market, in the form envisaged by Mao and his intellectual peers and forebears, were as divergent as east and west, or river and mountain. To unite them together is as brazen as it is audacious – but it, and it alone, sustains the mighty paradox that is the PRC today. And there is little sign that it is about to disappear.

Paradox in the Streets of the PRC Today

Rem Koolhaas's book plots the impact of this contradictory ideological posture in the current arrangement of Chinese public space. The entities preceding the PRC, and the PRC for the first 40 years of its existence were agricultural societies. Even today, over a half of the PRC's population is still based in the countryside (a massive step from the three- quarters based in the countryside only a decade ago). But, as any visitor to the PRC in the last five years will know, the break off point between the countryside and the city is harder and harder to plot, with most rural areas looking very much like urban sprawl. With the added complication of a massive floating population (estimated at up to 200 million people at any one time), no one is quite sure who lives where, or whether the cities are winning over the countryside.

This becomes more marked when one looks simply at the arrangement of city space. In 2005, a Party Secretary of a city in northern PRC airily told me that the trouble with Europeans was that they made decisions far too slowly. 'Look at me', he said, forking precious abalone into his mouth, 'I can say, Build this place, and it will be up in a few months. If there is somewhere in the way, fine, I tell them to tear it down. These days, a building over five years old is regarded as an ancient monument'. He then went off to preside over the groundbreaking ceremony for a new, dazzling Public Security Bureau office. This was to match the equally gleaming, intimidating City Offices that had been thrown up a couple of years before.

---

9   Rem Koolhass ed *et al*, *Great Leap Forward*, New York 2001.

Modern PRC cities have a sameness about them, in the architectural designs and in the layout, that strikes most visitors. It used to be that there was a uniform scrappiness about the centre of the PRC's great urban places. 24/7 chaos reigned around Beijing's Train Station, the usual embarkation point for those arriving (planes were relatively rare even a decade ago). Guangzhou was little better. Foreigners arriving would be swamped by people offering hotels, taxis and guide services. These days, such areas have been cleaned up and are under greater control. Beijing Station has a pleasant concourse, which is hardly ever heaving with people. You can even book train tickets online rather than fighting ten rounds with the 1,000 strong queue in front of you to get to the ticket window.

Because of the flexible planning regulations alluded to by the Party Secretary I talked to in 2005, setting out the city space is fairly easy. Roads are ploughed through residential areas where they need to be, people are moved out of their homes and shifted into the new residential areas, at the edges of cities. In Beijing there have been some bitter disputes between long-term residents about this, but on the whole the process is brutally short. Compensation is paid, and people are simply moved on. Buildings are chucked up with workers scrambling over them in bamboo-constructed scaffolding, barely cognizant of health or safety requirements (despite the fact that, in law at least, the PRC has pretty good legislation in this area. It's just hardly ever implemented). There is the gleaming example of Shenzhen, bordering Hong Kong, and mentioned later in this book. Shenzhen was built not quite in a day, but pretty close to it. Of the new skyscrapers and offices, an eighth of those built in the early 1980s either simply fell down or suffered major structural problems.[10] This didn't stop the second Great Leap Forward from surging ahead, with yet more buildings being put up, so that at any one time only half the office space in the city was in use. Many visits to other cities familiarized me with the peculiar existential emptiness of new Chinese offices. The old work unit spaces had at least a lived-in feel about them, even if it always seemed life was about to move on. There were usually a few piles of old newspapers, pens, a water container, and from time to time a stove on which a kettle was boiling. In the new blocks, things look clean, and there is endless space, punctuated by the occasional living body. But the whole environment is pervaded by a thin, intangible layer of building dust, like the place has never quite recovered from the unsettlement of the big bang of its construction, and this cosmic material will forever circulate these spaces, waiting for the expected activity to arrive.

---

10 Koolhaas, p 245.

This is one of the more concrete contradictions of the new PRC – the puzzling inactivity and emptiness at the heart of all the chaotic movement. The other is the veneer of organization and arrangement over this space – the cities with their development zones, university zones, business zones, and residential zones – all indicating a neat level of development, and supporting the notion that this whole environment is in fact following the robust ideology of the socialist market economy. But, it seems these props don't really add together. The development zones, for instance, set off from the main economic effort of the city like the old foreign trade compounds in Canton in the mid nineteenth century, when segregation was so de rigeur that the Chinese authorities forbade foreigners who could speak any Chinese being based there. In fact, the modern development zones are so amorphous and vague that their subsidiaries reach deep into the other parts of the city. Universities need to be roped into their activity, people from the residential areas work in them, the same process of separation of people from their place of work as has been the case in the West for many decades has now occurred in the PRC, giving birth to that other fine import, urban rush hours. It makes the more cynical wonder whether the business zones are not, in fact, hyper-work units modelled on the old '*danweis*' that structured Chinese life for almost half a century, only privatized and accommodating more diverse populations and of course, sensitive to market, not socialist, imperatives.

There is something deeply fictional about these inter-urban divisions. While they seem to indicate firm control and organization, in fact all they show are arbitrary divisions, underneath which something very much like the organic cities of the west, where functions of places are mixed up, seems to exist. They also imply a level of planning and approval that, infamously, simply doesn't exist. As the Party Secretary in the northern city I referred to above illustrated, applying to build, then constructing, even the most monumental structures in the PRC is frequently down to the say-so of one man. A powerful example of this was the Beijing Opera House, now being completed beside the Great Hall of the People in the dead centre of Beijing. A 'competition' was held in 2000 to select the most appropriate design. The French plan, which finally won, was not the most popular, and indeed the announcement of its success caused dozens of eminent Chinese architects to protest. Their opposition had reason. What was the point of building a huge glass ball in a semi-lake in one of the dustiest cities on the planet? And how did it blend in with the more conservative structures around it? But the then President, Jiang Zemin was taken by the design, and in the end that was enough to push it through. The fine divisions and plots of Chinese cities, therefore, are somewhat misleading. There are few properly implemented procedures for putting up buildings, in any design, of any size, anywhere (despite what the regulations might say). Nor are there protections for those places already standing. More often than not, the whim of a powerful official to leave his (or, very rarely, her) mark on the landscape means that a place is built, and the site chosen for it has everything there ripped away. The ultimate example of this is the destruction of almost all of Beijing's ancient city walls on the instructions of Mao Zedong in the early 1950s, motivated simply by his quest to build a 'modern' and therefore in his mind Soviet style city.

Public and Private in the New PRC

Material, visible contradictions are one thing. But, in the New PRC the invisible contradictions run the deepest. Perhaps the most elemental of these is the division of public and private, both in terms of the economy, and of people's lives. Until the 1980s, the Chinese economy was wholly state run. There was little incentive for people to do their own thing – and in fact, in most areas, particularly towards the end of Mao's reign, people were actually blankly prohibited from being independent.

The real start of the Reform and Opening Up Process in late 1978 was the setting up of the household responsibility system, where farmers were simply allowed to sell surplus crops back to the state for a small profit. This single spark provoked the prairie fire that rages to this day. In the mid 1980s, a whole process of privatizing companies was started, with people being freed up, if they chose, to do their own thing. This process continued throughout the 1990s. In 2002, entrepreneurs were actually allowed to join the Party, and in 2003 the private sector was formally recognized in the new revised Chinese constitution. The Organization for Economic Cooperation and Development (OECD), in their first official report on the Chinese economy in 2005 admitted that the private sector contributed to more than half of the Chinese development rate over the last few years.[11]

But in fact, things are not so simple. The pleasing initial contradiction between private and public, which tidies up at least some of the grey area of where the government operates and where the private individual is free, dissolves a little when one looks more carefully at what has actually been happening over the last two decades. This is ably done in a recent book by

11 OECD, Economic Survey of China 2005. http://www.oecd.org/document/21/0,2340,en_2649_34571_35331797_1_1_1,00.html (accessed 28 March 2006).

Standard Chartered economist, Stephen Green and academic Guy Liu Shaojia.[12] A huge number of companies have been 'privatised' and shifted to the private sector since the 1980s. And it is true that the traditional work units have been radically reformed, with the loss making parts hived off. Many State Owned Enterprises (SOEs) have been floated on the various stock exchanges in Shanghai, Shenzhen and Beijing. Some have even been floated abroad, in London or on National Association of Securities Dealers Automated Quotations (NASDAQ) in the US. But as Green and Liu's book shows, tracing back the share ownership of a lot of these companies reveals that for many of them, the government is still the majority shareholder. The famous 'cage' that Chen Yun, economist and political sparring mate of Deng Xiaoping in the 1980's talked about, within which the bird of the economy would be able to flutter, still looks like it is there.

This is important because it touches on other areas of so-called liberalization in China. And these, too, look deeply contradictory. In 1995, I was told by a young Party member that, of course, it was absolutely fine in the PRC to say that you did not agree or support the Communist Party. Only you couldn't do anything about this. In effect, you were free to say things, but not to do anything. A decade later, it is widely accepted that you can sit and talk all you like in the various Starbucks and coffee shops throughout Beijing about the terrible things the Party has done, and how it should pack up and stand down – but to go into print about this is to tread firmly over the line. You are free, but within very definite limits. And sometimes, those limits can be arbitrarily drawn very close to you.

The Biggest Contradiction of All

The fundamental contradiction of the modern Chinese state is simply this. The Party is rolling back the frontiers of the state, and disappearing from many areas of life that it was once prevalent in – but it is still ubiquitous and everywhere. The Party proclaims an ideology that everyone must agree with, and no one believes in, including, it is very much suspected, most of the Party officials mandated with upholding this ideology. The zoned self reflects the zoned city – neatly delineated areas for the modern Chinese to function through and exist in, with some areas freely accessible, and others off-limits. In the intellectual landscape one is as chaperoned as in the physical one, with a veneer of control underwritten by what looks very much

---

12 *Exit the Dragon: Privatisation and State Control in China,* London and Oxford 2005.

like anarchy and chaos. In the PRC, we have gone from the outright banning of the music of Beethoven during the CR, to one of the world's leading centres of avant-garde art. This ranges from the metal curtain on which was hung living insects which slowly died and decomposed, exhibited a few years back in Beijing, to the absolute extreme of a Chinese artist whose work consisted of him making a prostitute pregnant, then aborting the foetus and photographing himself eating this – about as extreme and revolting a statement of the nihilism some feel in contemporary China. Visitors to the Xinhua bookshops in the main centres of Chinese urban life can pick up good translations of *Ulysses*, most of the Western canon, and a plethora of up-to-date economics, political and sociological treatises. The works of Foucault, Bourdieu, Amartya Sen and Noam Chomsky are all widely available. To this day, Chinese is the only language into which the complete works of philosopher Ludwig Wittgenstein have been translated (there is as yet no complete English edition of his works – some still remain in his native German) – a feat achieved by Professor Jiang Yi of Beijing University, whose ceremony marking the completion of this great project in 2003 I attended in Beijing.

Chinese news programmes are highly informative about most foreign affairs, and domestic Chinese economic developments. But, stray into one of the forbidden areas, and suddenly the landscape changes. It feels a bit like looking at the Google Earth website, where some places are shown with remarkable clarity, only for one to come across a sensitive site (usually in the US or the UK) which is blurred and imprecise. The map of permissible topics in the media in the PRC is a similar mixture of the blurred and obscured. Talk about, for instance, the handling of Taiwan and Mainland Chinese relations, or the treatment of forbidden sects like Falungong, or how to deal with restive Chinese national minorities, like the Tibetans, or the Uiguar over in Xinjiang, becomes a formulaic ritual, where the intellectual shutters come down.

There are myriads of other contradictions. This is a developing country, where the system is awash with money, and where the cities are heaving with newly wealthy people – and yet, it also contains almost 100 million citizens who earn less than a dollar a day, a paradox neatly encapsulated by the US Council of International Relations by the statement that New China was on its way to becoming the world's first 'rich poor' country.[13] It's a country which prides itself on tradition and history, but in which the

---

13 *China: The Balance Sheet*, Washington 2006.

landscape in most cities is barely ten years old. It is a culture capable of the most searing expressions of artistic sensibility, producing some of the greatest poetry and material art the world has ever seen, and at the same time artefacts of colossal vulgarity (witness the wooden statues of large bellied Buddhas that can be found in many high class Chinese hotels, or the utter crassness of most contemporary Chinese pop music).

It is a country that is as fervently puritanical as it is sensual and excessive. Look for the Chinese version of the newsagent top shelf, or cable TV porn, and you will look in vain. This is one market that *Playboy* magazine has yet to penetrate. But on the other hand, in a way far more openly than in the UK or the US, prostitutes ply their trade in most of the hotels and bars in Beijing and other cities, occasionally swept up by 'Strike Hard' campaigns. *The Economist* argued in 2001 that the sex sector was the one enjoying the most rapid growth in the PRC. It has led to an AIDS explosion, and a sense of complete moral disorientation.

Atop all these minor contradictions sits the final one. This is a country of great diversity, but at the moment stuck with a limited and rigid political system. There is an argument, one often used by more urbane Chinese apologists (frequently by those who have studied abroad, and therefore become much more effective defenders of their country's current system) that the very reason why the PRC has such a rigid system is that giving voice to all of these different perspectives and available minorities would be unworkable. Democracy would fall at the first hurdle through overload. Such arguments sometimes take a more sinister term. Basically, you will be told, the Party is the only option at the moment because of the number of uneducated, poor quality people there still are, people who cannot possible understand the idea of voting, and who need a couple of generations more 'improvement' to be worthy of this honour.

The Reappearance of Class

The Party might represent all, but visitors over the last half-century to the various phases that the PRC has been through have all been struck by how hierarchical it has remained. With each new phase of development, a new elite appears. This can be called the Paradox of Chinese class. Mao may have been aiming for a programme of social equality, and a rooting out of the old divisions and inequities, but what he achieved was to empower a new group of elite cadres who ran the country round them, often to their own benefit. Mao was aware that his various attempts to address this before had not been successful when, in 1966, he made rooting out bureaucratism one of the key objectives of the organized chaos of the CR, attacking the very establishment of the Party and its vested interests. The CR period did see a degree of egalitarianism – something looked back on nostalgically by some veterans of that time. But it seems that Orwell was right in his fable, *Animal Farm*: given a chance, elites will always reappear. In the CR, there were hierarchies amongst Red Guards and Rebellious Groups, there were subtle gradations within those groups, and a pecking order between different regions, who competed with each other to demonstrate allegiance and adherence to Mao. Nor was it simply that the previous cadre elite were dumped and a new elite, born from the proletariat and working classes, replaced them. As American academic, Lynn T White showed in a study of the CR period on Shanghai, on the whole children of high ranking cadres were the most active Red Guards, and promoted their interests very effectively – with the so-called recipients of the CR political programme, workers and their children, frequently being the victims of campaigns.[14]

Hierarchy is embedded in the egalitarian, one Party state that has maintained its existence to this day. Any visitor to the PRC who has attended formal dinners will know about the tremendous kafuffle before people take their seats at even a simple dinner. There is a careful geography of power being decoded at each of these events, something that has to be understood instinctively. It is not solely about age, Party rank, or wealth, though each of these is factored in. It seems to be a sort of Chinese X factor. Some have status, and some don't. Interpreting this takes good intuitive skills.

Such sense of hierarchy, side by side with imprecations to serve the people, maintained to this day, and a careful choreography of equality where officials ostensibly get paid small wages, and live in compounds like the bulk of the rest of the population, comes across in almost all areas of life in the PRC. In academic life, in business life, in political life, hierarchy spreads and stretches it wings. Even the seeming 'letting way' by the more powerful to the less is significant because they have the ability to act like this. Chinese Vice President, Zeng Qinghong, one of the nine most powerful men in contemporary China (he is a permanent member of the Politburo, the apex of political decision making) is famed for his 'self-effacing' manner, and for insisting at one meeting once that a humble worker have the comfortable seat while he sat on a stool. Such theatrical displays only show that people's awareness of hierarchy in the PRC, and of those who have and do not have power, is highly developed. That whole issue will be looked at later in this book.

---

14 *Policies of Chaos,* Princeton, 1989.

'You Can't Keep a Good Man Down': the Continuing Influence of Mao

The final word on contradictions has to be a tribute to Mao. In these days where his image seems to be fading, and his influence at last falling away, one has to admit that making contradictions the central tenet of his philosophy was not such a bad idea. It meant that he could encapsulate the impossible paradoxes that made up his, and now our, modern PRC. The answer to the questions about what China we mean when we talk about China becomes a little easier to answer thanks to help from Mao – we just have to accept contradictions. And we shouldn't be surprised if the China of the future is also, in many ways, contradictory. The price of consistency would be far too high – the effective dissolution of the country.

CHAPTER FOUR:
THE HISTORY GAME

One part of received wisdom about China is that it is a place where history lies heavy. It lives in the streets, in people's minds, in their hearts and their language. The purported 5,000 years of tradition and continuous civilization is in the air that the Chinese breathe. But, as there are many Chinas, so there are also many histories. Since 1949, history has been an important zone to control, and the interpretation and meaning of events has been set and reset according to the political winds. In that sense, history in the PRC is just as much a game as politics, and every bit as high- risk. As in so many other places, history is often as much about the present as about the past. And, as some events of the PRC's recent past will become less important over the years, others are likely to resurface. 40 years after it started, I would say that the CR is one seminal event that will increase in importance in the years ahead, and for that reason deserves far closer attention.

The CR: The Basics

Before even beginning to talk about the immense complexity of the CR itself, just addressing how long it ran throws up some immediate challenges. The usual dates neatly fit into the final ten years of Mao Zedong's life − 1966 to 1976. Ten Years of Chaos, or the Ten Turbulent Years, as one account of the period states in its title.[1] But in fact, there are good arguments to say that the CR ran for only three years till 1969, when the Ninth Party Congress in April of that year (the first Party Congress for over a decade) ended the real excesses of the rebellious groups, and reined in the provinces which were getting most out of control. The seven years after then were an extended coda, dealing with the political fallout of the first three years, and

---

1   For instance, the title of Yan Jiaqi and Gao Gao's *Turbulent Decade: A History of the Cultural Revolution*, Hawaii 1996.

themselves constituting a wholly separate movement, the culmination of which was the death of heir apparent, Lin Biao in 1971, and the various machinations around Mao leading up to his own death in September 1976.

If we take the three years of what we can call the CR proper (or the shorter CR), 1966 to 1969, we can see radical differences in how the movement was conducted across the country. For Beijing, while there were extensive rallies, and mass mobilizations, the main meat of the movement was the political infighting within the central leadership, between those perceived as reformists, and those who were agitating for greater fidelity to Maoism, or at least what was asserted as Maoism at the time. The impact of this trickled across the country, but its manifestation differed from province to province. In Inner Mongolia, it took a particularly virulent turn, leading to an all out purge against cadres of Mongolian ethnicity (estimates of up to 100 thousand deaths have been given for those who died over this period in the region, though the official figure is only 16 thousand). A similar trend occurred in Xinjiang, where Muslims were forced to eat pork, and accused of harbouring treacherous intent towards the central, predominantly Han, state. Tibet offered a further variation – where radical rebellious groups of Tibetan ethnicity sought to prove their political credentials by turning upon their own culture, bombing lama temples and closing down thousands of Tibet's monasteries.[2]

Elsewhere in the PRC, while the ethnic dimension may have been lacking, there were fierce tribal and social clashes. The central city of Wuhan in Hubei Province, scene of the famous incident that almost led to civil war in 1967, saw the army pitted against students – two of the most favoured social groups. Shanghai saw the establishment, in early 1968, of Paris style communes, which were to be the expression of purest commune-ism, but were vetoed by the central leadership as anti-revolutionary (refusing to accept the authority of anyone except Mao). Guangzhou, deep in the south, grew so restive that there were fears that it would split away from the country and create a new, independent entity – a rumour that was bolstered

---

2   See Chapter Twelve of UK based Tibetan historian Tsering Shakya's balanced *The Dragon in the Land of Snows, a History of Modern Tibet Since 1947* London 1999. Tibet deserves a whole chapter on its own, both because of the extremes it seems to push people to – either acceptance of the Chinese hard line on the region being an inalienable part of Chinese territory, despite the flimsiest historical evidence for this (Shakya goes into this in detail) or wholly purblind romanticizing of the issue, exemplified in Hollywood films like the adaptation of recently deceased Nazi, Helmut Harrer's 1950s account, *Seven Years in Tibet.*

by the tale that Lin Biao had his sights on this area as a place of refuge when he fled Beijing in 1971.

This difference in the nature of the CR in the PRC's various geographies is compounded by the immensity of the movement – a campaign that drew in hundreds of millions of people, touching the lives of almost every Chinese person alive at that time. Every area of life, private and public, was saturated by idol worship of Mao, and with rituals to demonstrate fidelity to him. Mao's works, his words, were ubiquitous. There was a profound mobilization of society. But, people's individual experiences of this period were to be very different. Some suffered very badly, others entered into it with deep fervour and commitment, while others were hardly affected at all.

The Benefits of the CR

The common perception is that the CR was a disaster, ten wasted years, in which a holocaust was visited upon the Chinese people. Apportioning of blame to this day is a delicate issue. The Gang of Four are usually cited as the main fall guys, though there is wide recognition, in the right form of words, that Mao Zedong was the chief inspiration. Official judgement on the movement delivered in 1981 was simply that the CR was a mistake, a good amount of the '30%' bad that Mao Zedong was judged to have done.[3]

This sits uneasily on the fact that, as the late writer Ba Jin was the first of many to comment, the CR was a movement that attracted great mass appeal, and involved far more perpetrators than victims. To mention the CR now to people in the PRC, is to attract a number of responses. Younger people who were not born at the time might know about it vaguely as a harsh and fanatical period. Older participants may declare weary horror, or even offer their own account of the upheavals of that time. Some might take the nostalgic tack, looking back at the general equality in society then, and gently referring to their innocent exploits in the naïve, gung-ho Red Guard groups. But there are few that will openly admit that they participated in struggle sessions against victims, denounced teachers, or even held responsibility for one of the millions of acts of violence, many leading up to death, that occurred. When the subject of the CR comes up, the real activists fall silent.

---

3   'The Resolution on Certain Historical Questions in the History of our Party since the Founding of the People's Republic of China' issued by the CPC in 1981.

Reading contemporary accounts of the CR, however, at least during what can be called its 'red hot' phase, one is struck by the way in which it captured the imagination of a mass audience, and has some claims to be a genuinely popular movement. Certainly, the attack on the establishment, on bureaucracy and entrenched self-interest groups touched a popular chord. As did the general attempt to eradicate inequalities. Respected academics like Jiangxi-born, but now Australia-based Mobo Gao, have argued persuasively that the political legacy of the CR was genuinely democratic.[4] There were attempts to empower the least privileged groups, and an attack on what was seen as the age-old cancers of Chinese society, corruption and elitism, with a tiny number controlling resources. Party interests were challenged. Women, peasants and workers enjoyed positive discrimination. In the plethora of Red Guard Group publications there were a range of voices and perspectives that were not allowed space before, and haven't been since – something close to a genuine pluralism. Many members of society were encouraged to be politically active. The legacy of the CR cannot be wholly dismissed. The current top leadership of the PRC all cut their political teeth during the CR period. The experience of it has given them a realism that those younger lack.

This is by no means to denigrate the enormous dislocation and social damage the movement caused. Mao's invocation to his followers that, without destruction there could be no creation led to a wholesale, and indiscriminate attack on anything construed as part of the 'old culture' – temples, works of art, works of literature. For ten years, at least in terms of fiction and poetry, the PRC was silenced. National treasures like the Forbidden Palace were saved only by the intervention of top leaders. But commentators nowadays have noted that the current 'development' spree, which the PRC has enjoyed for the last two decades, has posed a far greater risk to its so-called traditional material and intellectual culture. The *hutongs* of Beijing were razed by the need to create a twenty-first century city, ready for the 2008 Olympics, not the marauding Red Guards of three decades ago. And the wholesale reconstruction of most of the PRC's cities has been done under the imperatives of the socialist market economy, not ideological Maoism.

It is easy to see why there are so many who are still vaguely nostalgic of the CR period. However, selective their memories, Chinese society then did

---

4   'Debating the Cultural Revolution: Do We Only Know What we Believe', *Critical Asian Studies*, No 34.

not have the huge inequalities and disequilibrium that it does now. An older cadre who had weathered the CR in Inner Mongolia, one of the worst affected areas, did say to me once that in terms of the socialist project, parts of the CR made sense – the desire to eradicate inequality, to create a level playing field for everyone, to make the Party the servant of the people rather than the other way around. The volte-face committed after Mao's death in 1976, however unavoidable, was deeply puzzling to the real vanguard of the revolution who felt that it negated all their suffering and sacrifice to see the reappearance of the same kinds of privilege and inequality that they had laboured for so long to get rid of. In that sense the CR offers an either-or scenario. If what you are after is real Maoism, then this is what it looked like. Complete organization of social life, almost approaching communism, rigid ideological control and a level social playing field. Contemporary PRC, for most of the actors in this enormous play, is a scarier, more insecure place. The old, 'dog-eat-dog' spirit that dominated before the revolution in 1949 has returned. There are the obscenely wealthy ranged against those with absolutely nothing. And for those that do fall through the social security net, there is precious little help on offer for them.

Uncovering CR History in the PRC

The more interesting aspect of the CR for those looking at contemporary PRC, and its lessons for what history means in the current society, however, is the way in which the CR is both misremembered, and disremembered. There is, of course, the issue of what can be known about the CR for those either growing up in the PRC now, or coming to the subject new. Say you stop in a mid-size Chinese provincial city, and are interested in researching what happened during the CR there. Almost certainly, depending on who you are, your interest will arouse questions, and a certain level of suspicion. There will be an inevitable defensiveness, if you are a foreigner. A reaction along the lines of, Ah, here comes another outsider trying to dig up something bad about the great society we have built, and denigrating the PRC's face. This reaction is built on two great constants of the modern PRC – the first the belief, universally accepted now, that the CR was bad and a somewhat shameful thing, and therefore best left forgotten, and the second that any attempt to look at what is regarded as negative is therefore a violation of the socially accepted vision of the PRC's 'face' – a mass distortion of the individual 'faces' that people are so careful to protect, and which outsiders are often told they have no way to understand.

For those that have the time and effort to penetrate this initial Great Wall of suspicion, there will then be a more practical issue. Where are the archives or the material residue of evidence for the CR? The brave can front up at the various, and increasingly grand looking 'public libraries' in the PRC. They can request to wade through whatever contemporary material might be available there. They might get sight of newspapers, but the information in these will be limited. The really lucky (I was one) might locate a stash of the many hundreds of Red Guard pamphlets, and stencilled news-sheets from some friendly source. But it is unlikely a library would either have many of these, or if it did, would allow access to them. Even in the days of the information superway, there are some clear 'No Entry' signs posted to block access. The excuse would probably be that these are unimportant or squalid little pieces, not worthy of genuine, serious research.

For those mad enough to think they might be able to look at restricted material, I guess the advice is that, of course, it never harms to ask – and maybe one day one of the many thousands of requests might lead somewhere. But so far, no one has succeeded. In theory, the so-called 'Red Top' bulletins issued to Party Members, and the minutes of internal meetings should be released under the 30-year rule. But as an enormous and ill-defined array of documents is considered 'restricted' in the PRC, what material, if any, is released is amongst the most asinine and uncontentious. The real documents, chronicling the real events, are safely under lock and key, and likely to remain so for the foreseeable future.

Some Chinese researchers, like Ye Yongli, based in Shanghai, have managed to gain enough trust from high-level political supporters to get a peek into the archive. He has written biographies of the Gang of Four, and books about aspects of the CR. But his works fit neatly into the current ideological parameters of the Party, and have been carefully vetted. Failing either a regime change, or a dazzling about-face by the leaders at the moment, the archives both nationally and provincially are unlikely to open up. A further practical point, once more best exemplified by looking at the case of Inner Mongolia, is simply that the really sensitive material was shifted from the provinces to the central archives in the early 1980s, never to be returned. The central government was not going to relinquish control over such an important area as free dissemination of historical knowledge, especially once the consensus had been accepted that the CR was a shameful disaster and should therefore be condemned, and forgotten.

The Chinese Poet and the CR

The only other option for someone in this position who does wish to find out what happened then is simply to try and talk to people. Anyone over their mid-forties would have some memories of the CR period, and people over retirement age would have probably participated in it to some degree, as either activists (statistically most likely) or victims. But here a very strange thing happens. For a decade, I was trying to talk to people about the CR. I did it first in Inner Mongolia, and then in Beijing. At the beginning, I usually found that I kept running up against a wall. I was either told by those who said they were my 'true friends' that the CR was way off-limits, and that apart from them, I should not talk about this issue with anyone else. Then they would, depending on what specific favours they needed from me, drip-feed me with information they had. There were more interesting responses. An initial hesitance, a sort of verbal flick of the wrist, 'Oh, so you are interested in *that*', a knowing look, but with a little hint of worry. And then, a bit further on, a sort of guilty stare, and a 'the CR was a great mistake' homily, and then, silence. The very inarticulacy of these people was atypical. Why the need for silence? Pointed questions about whether the CR had had much of an impact locally were usually met with more frostiness, and a surge of generalizations, 'Oh, the CR saw a lot of public meetings, a lot of mass-mobilizations, yes, we were all Mao's little red soldiers then'. This response seemed very strange. What specifically had happened? Who had been victims, who protagonists?

There was one occasion when the discomfort of the person I was talking to went beyond this to something much more jarring. He was a poet, based then in the city of Guangzhou, who I met with a friend while staying there for a month in late 1994. He was living in an army compound. His daughter had gone to the UK to study. He wore a slick black polo neck jumper. When I first talked to him in his living room he seemed distracted and edgy. He sat on the edge of the sofa, fidgeting, while his wife prepared dinner. I heard he had written a few poetic dramas, but when I asked, he said that these had all been produced in the early 1970s. This intrigued me, as very few writers had been active then. Over dinner, he got increasingly drunk, toasting me with white spirit every five minutes, demanding we declare our friendship, becoming almost aggressive in his hospitality. The very mention of the CR seemed to trip him up, making him sink down more white spirit, plying more on me. His hospitality got so aggressive, my friend and I decided to bolt. At the door, he followed up behind us, and produced an odd, half dismissive, half bitter grunt. 'The CR,' he declared, 'who's interested in that?'

A few weeks later, still clutching the book of his poetic works he had given me when sober, I showed it to another friend in the town where I was living. She was a Chinese literature teacher. His name seemed to be familiar to her.

She pulled down a great dictionary of modern Chinese writers, and then grunted in triumph. 'Yes, it is him,' she said, 'he was one of the writers chosen to work with the Gang of Four. No wonder.' She looked at his book distastefully. 'A collaborator.' So, I thought, I had seen my first properly exposed perpetrator, rather than one of the legions of victims I had been familiar with up till then.

There were a few others, of course. In the flat next to one of my best friends', there was a man who was widely known within the college in which he worked to have been one of the most enthusiastic persecutors of those deemed to belong to the 'black five classes' of the CR period. People didn't treat him differently, and he didn't seem to suffer from any overt discrimination or prejudice – but it was clear that there was a certain aura about him, and he was treated with caution and reserve. At the beginning, I couldn't work out why he hadn't been banged up, or simply ostracized. But then someone explained it to me. There were too many like him. When the CR was finally over and done with, and some form of retribution and re-evaluation was achieved, it wasn't an option to cart off another generation of damned and condemned. That had, after all, been happening for the last ten years. The only workable way forward was for people to return to their work places, and, despite what had been going on, and who had committed which crimes against whom, simply get on with life again. Desires and feelings for revenge simply needed to be suppressed.

The CR must have had a colossal toll on the mental well-being and the psychological health of those who had been through it, as did the great cover-up afterwards. What came across in descriptions of the movement by participants, victims, and onlookers afterwards was the spiritual rather than physical toll the movement took. This is best captured by one of the finest accounts of the period, Yang Jiang's *A Cadre Life in Six and a Half Chapters*, which, for all its aching brevity, distils much of the intellectual's experience of the period. Yang, and her husband, the great writer Qian Zhongshu, had both been educated abroad, in the UK and Europe. They were polyglots, who had translated some of the major western works of literature (including Cervantes) into Chinese. Qian, before the 1949 revolution, had written *Fortress Besieged (Wei Cheng)*, still regarded as one of the finest novels to be produced by a Chinese writer in the modern era, a work starkly different from most other modern Chinese novels for its use of light irony and sophisticated wordplay (the inevitable impact of Maoism on literature in the PRC has been, until recently, a grinding social realism – replaced in the last decade by savage cynicism or market-orientated pulp fiction).[5] They had all the ingredients that would have made them deeply suspect in Mao's China. Experience abroad and sophisticated (for which read unreliable) political opinions. In the CR, they were sent from Beijing to a cadre school, set up in 1969 to 're-educate' intellectuals and expose them to the experiences of peasants. Such schools were primitive and harsh, places where the inmates were expected to perform hard physical labour. Not surprisingly, they appeared much like concentration camps, even if the majority of the inmates were to survive.

Yang's account contains one telling scene where a doctor, examining her husband, Qian, emaciated after months of poor food and hard labour, notes that he has the same name as the great writer, and laughs, unaware that in fact Qian is the great writer, only reduced to something barely human. Returning to the work camp, however, Qian is approached by a dog that still recognizes him from his smell from the first day he had arrived there, the one part of his old self he seems to have kept. Yang's conclusion is clear. In the CR, people were reduced to the level where fellow human beings did not recognize them but animals could. The Tianjin writer, Sun Li, wrote a similarly dark tale about life in the CR, a short story about a man banged up in a commune with other 'black classes' who comes close to committing suicide, such is the despair he is reduced to, till his life is literally saved by a member of the so-called 'bad classes', a fortune teller incarcerated with him for carrying out superstitious practices, who reads his face and tells him that this dark period of his life will soon be over, one of the few moments that gives him hope. Sun Li's grim final comment is that, at a time of shrill political judgement and denunciation, his saviour was not the Party, which had set itself up as the giving of all things good, but by a person condemned as a cheat and swindler.

The CR as a Spiritual Holocaust

Spiritual holocaust seems a better way to describe the CR than holocaust proper, though this is the term that some Chinese commentators have used.

---

5   Published in English translation by Penguin in 2005. See also Julia Lovell's interesting study, *The Politics of Cultural Capital – China's Quest for a Nobel Prize in Literature*, Hawaii 2006 for a discussion the general lack of engagement by Western critics in Chinese literature, and the reciprocating (perhaps resulting) sense of cultural inferiority felt by most Mainland writers after 1949.

While it is true there were high levels of violence in the CR, and a large number of fatalities, the main thrust of the campaign was simply to eradicate certain types of thinking, and to victimize designated bad classes. The CR, to those on the outside, looks a mysterious event. Something based on the elliptical, opaque thoughts of an increasingly senile, paranoid leader, cooped up in his compound, disgruntled, according to accounts afterwards, by how the revolution he had nurtured and led was getting away from him. But in terms of the overall narrative of Chinese history created after 1949, the CR makes perfect sense, and had a terrible inevitability from the late 1950s, as Harvard based historian of China, Roderick MacFarquhar has made clear in a monumental three volume study of the period leading up to 1966.[6] In terms of a political movement, there were tensions within the leadership in Beijing from the 1950s, and a number of false steps, the most disastrous of which was the Great Leap Forward, an event that is claimed by writers like Jasper Becker and others to have led to the deaths of up to 30 million people during the great famine from 1957 to 1960.[7] The disaster of collectivization should have humbled Mao, but as has been noted frequently since, there was simply no mechanism to get rid of the father of the revolution, and while he may, in his own words, have been parked like a Buddha on a shelf, leaving the running of the country to the two capable technocrats, Liu Shaoqi and Deng Xiaoping, he never went away.

Mao subscribed to a very particular view of history, and to his own special place in it. He was, as he was fond of saying, the unifier of China, the new China, paralleling the bloody career of the fabled (perhaps even mythical) first emperor Qin Shihuang. But he had also cobbled together a Marxist vision of social progress, and tied this up with a fervent nationalism (proving Clement Atlee's words that if you scratch a communist you'll find a nationalist underneath). The Great Leap Forward was inspired by the desire to overtake the UK's steel production in three years. The PRC was a great power and deserved more respect from the community of nations. This fitted with a history of humiliations and defeats, visited on the Qing Dynasty at the hands of foreign powers in the nineteenth century, and focussed on the pivotal events of the Opium Wars, and then the Boxer Rebellions and the sacking of Beijing by the allied powers. Mao's celebrated comment in 1949 about the PRC at last standing up (one of the few sentences he was ever recorded speaking) cemented this national myth.

---

6   *The Origins of the Cultural Revolution*, Oxford, 1974, 1987, 1997, Vol. I, Vol. II, & Vol. III.
7   *Hungry Ghosts: Mao's Secret Famine*, London 1996.

On some levels, then, the CR can be seen as one of a number of campaigns that preserve the integrity of this national narrative – part of a battle of the good classes against the bad, pitting the supporters of the revolution against its detractors. It was also a further piece of unfinished business – a revisiting of the divisions and tensions that had existed in Chinese society before the CR, the resolution of which had been put on hold. Far from being unified, Chinese society had been riddled with social, ethnic and cultural divisions. The CR was one of the means of trying to forge some unity. The battles of the CR were to pit the favoured classes against the condemned, working out a grand moral vector that was part of the plan for a perfect society.

Because many of the archival materials for the CR period are now inaccessible, and it is so difficult to look into what people remember of this period, a comprehensive history either by a foreigner or a Chinese is still some way off. Gao Gao and Yan Jiaqi, two Beijing based historians, made a brave attempt to write the *Ten Year History* in the late 1980s, but this was banned almost the moment it was produced, and both of the writers had to flee China after the Tiananmen Square Massacre (euphemistically called the 4 June Incident) in 1989.[8] In the West, scholars have laboured on various aspects of the CR – on provincial manifestations, on particular political aspects, on the 'eight model operas', on the few theatre pieces produced during this period, etc. But for a systematic account of the period, there has been little.[9] Of course, to be able to make sense of such a complex movement, with all the required documents, would need an army of researchers, working in a more sympathetic and open environment than prevails in the PRC now. We can safely say that for the moment, the full history of the CR is therefore simply unwriteable, and the government has succeeded in its efforts to push attention on, and let the ten years be not only ones of chaos, but of forgetfulness.

---

8 Translated as *Turbulent Decade: A History of the Great Cultural Revolution*, Hawaii Press 1996.
9 Roderick MacFarquhar and Michael Schoenhals have just produced *Mao's Final Revolution*, Harvard 2006, a general history of the CR, which partially starts to fill this enormous gap.

Specifics: The Case of the CR in Inner Mongolia

But the idea that the CR period can be put on the shelf and conveniently forgotten is not tenable. The CR is, in many areas, and for many people, a live issue. It formed them, created their world view, and the wounds, both physical and mental, that were suffered then are still not fully healed. The handling of the CR now, and the phenomenon of the movement itself, says a great deal about what kind of beast the PRC is, and what makes many people in it tick. The CR is not going to go away that easily.

Look at one specific area during the CR, and one specific period, that of the campaigns to root out the Inner Mongolia People's Party in the Inner Mongolia Autonomous Region in north-west China. According to the official statistics (and they are certainly underestimates) over 16 thousand people perished here from 1967 to 1969 as a result of the CR agitation. About a quarter of a million were wounded or injured. Many of these were of Mongolian ethnicity, which makes the CR as it manifested itself in this region have the characteristics of a genocidal movement.

The history is simple to set out. Inner Mongolia had been effectively ruled as a special region of China by a centrally appointed local government led by a local strongman, a Mongolian called Ulanfu. In 1966 during a meeting in Beijing, Ulanfu was judged to be unreliable, a practitioner of Soviet revisionism. There was a real bite to this sort of accusation in the area simply because of its proximity to the Mongolian People's Republic (MPR), a country that had been independent since 1921, but had been increasingly under Soviet control and influence. In the 1930s, it had suffered purges under its leader, Choibalsan, which had shown disturbing similarities to the Stalinist attacks being waged at the same time in the USSR. Many thousands of Buddhist monks had perished. Naturally, ethnic Mongolians in Inner Mongolia and what is still now popularly called Outer Mongolia enjoyed close links. The independence of the latter acted as an inspiration for those in Inner Mongolia who were rewarded, after their many years of waging revolution with the Chinese communists, with a highly ambiguous version of 'special autonomy', and an increasing campaign of internal migration by Han settlers (something that had, in fact, been ongoing for half a century).[10]

---

10 See Uradyn Bulag's, *The Mongols at China's Edge*, Boulder, Colorado 2002 for accounts of this.

By the time the USSR and the PRC had fallen out in the 1960s, therefore, any residual links between Mongolians either side of the border became a problem. Mongolians in the MPR were vassals of the evil Soviet revisionist empire, and contact with them meant immediate guilt by association. By the beginning of the CR, therefore, Chinese Mongolians were immediately suspect, and came under increasing pressure as the atmosphere became more paranoid. The suspicion, announced in 1967, after a series of local skirmishes involving the army and students, resulting in the death of a student in February 1967, became clear. In the 1930s and 1940s, during the great confusion of the anti-Japanese war, and the civil war with the Nationalists, there had been an Inner Mongolia People's Party. It had a clear intent to unify with the MPR to create a Pan- Mongolian state. That Party had continued to exist after 1949. Even worse, some of its members were active in the Chinese Communist Party, and cadres in the new system. Such treachery called for a mass campaign to dig them out.

No one was safe in such an environment. By the middle of 1968, hundreds of thousands of Mongolian cadres and herdsmen had been 'rooted out'. This involved varying levels of violence. One particularly grim account of a 'struggle session', recorded in Tumen and Zhu's 1995 Chinese language history of the CR in Inner Mongolia records how one man had his tongue ripped out, and another woman had her genitalia branded with red hot irons. Some herdsmen were roasted alive on grills.[11] A fictional account of the CR during this period, Ma Bo's, *Blood Red Sunset*, records how one man was driven to such despair that he ripped his own nails off.[12] Those perceived as intellectuals in Hohhot were struggled against in mass meetings, with many simply exiled to remote grassland areas.

By 1969, the new leadership imposed in the area in mid 1967 by Beijing had created so much chaos that the central government was again forced to intervene. General Teng Haiqing, the local strongman who had replaced Ulanfu, was removed from his positions and made to issue grovelling self-criticisms and apologies. After a few years of 're-education', he was to astonishingly resurface as a senior military leader in Jilin province, North East China, living on to 1996. At the April 1969 Ninth Party Congress, Mao Zedong demonstrated his power by simply issuing a single statement saying that 'mistakes in Inner Mongolia had been committed',demonstrating his

---

11 Tumen and Zhu Dongli, *Kang Sheng yu Neirendang de Anjian* (Kang Sheng and the Unjust Case of the Inner Mongolian People's Party) Beijing 1996.
12 Translated by Howard Goldblatt, Harmondsworth 1996.

dazzling ability to avoid all signs of personal involvement in the chaos that had been visited on the region. A large part of the region was split up into three areas, portioned out to other provinces (a move reversed in 1979) and a new leadership imposed in the small segment remaining. Like its population, what was left of Inner Mongolia in 1969 was feeble, truncated and compromised.

Part of the 'rectification process' in 1979 that took place after the formal ending of the Longer CR was for the Centre to admit that an 'Inner Mongolian People's Party' agitating for unification with the MPR had never actually existed. The whole tragedy was blamed simply on the 'Gang of Four and Lin Biao cliques'. But the Mongolians in the area, to this day, still regard the CR as clear evidence of the central government's suspicion of them, and its desire to see them totally assimilated. In the 1980s, resentment at the amount of violence in the CR period and the failure to hold anyone properly to account for this led to student demonstrations. These resurfaced inevitably in 1989, and again in the mid 1990s, when a local bookshop owner, Hada, was rewarded for his work of conducting cultural classes in the area by being jailed as a separatist for 15 years. He is still in jail to this day. The Mongolian anthropologist, Uradyn Bulag, now based in the US, has written about the kinds of identity allowed to national minorities in China and specifically about the permissible 'ethnic self-expressions' for Mongolians. Dressing up in colourful clothes, dancing exaggerated dances, eating mutton and drinking white spirit are all OK. But musing about just what the historical claims of the current Chinese state on Inner Mongolia are, or writing more trenchant articles in Chinese about the gradual annexation of the region, are good ways to be rewarded with unwanted police attention and very probably lengthy prison sentences.[13]

The local museum in Hohhot, housed at the moment in a handsome white building in the centre of the city opposite the government compound, is a metaphor of the treatment of the CR in a sensitive area. On the second floor of the building there is a display of 'Revolutionary History' recording the struggles against the Japanese and Nationalists in the region in the 1930s and 1940s. Ulanfu, since his rehabilitation, takes pride of place in this history. The establishment of the autonomous region in 1947 (two years before the creation of the PRC proper) is presented as a triumph for the PRC's inclusiveness and a symbol of the country's 'multi ethnic' composition. The years of reconstruction in the 1950s, when the herdlords,

---

13 Op. cit.

as they were called, were felled from power, are carefully documented. But come 1965, and silence falls on the exhibition. All there is now are various pictures of central leaders visiting the region from the late 1970s onwards, demonstrating their care and concern for the healthy development of the region, and their benevolent patronage of it.

Moving around Hohhot in 2005, searching for signs of the past, offers an interesting experience. Modern Hohhot has cleared out its 'old city' around the two temples in the west. The modern apartment blocks, roads and flyovers ubiquitous throughout the PRC run through the town. There are skyscrapers, a relatively new railway station, and an intimidating, large city hall on the road to the airport. In 2005, Hohhot enjoyed 35 per cent growth, due to domestic and foreign investment. The oldest buildings in the town date from barely two decades ago, and look about three times that age. Even the so-called Ming dynasty temple looks highly renovated. Searching for any traces of the violent movement that so affected the region from 1966 onwards in the material landscape is doomed to failure. Bookshops contain little, if any, material relating to the CR in Inner Mongolia. The second-hand bookshops around the university district sometimes throw up old Red Guard pamphlets, and the occasional underground account in Chinese of the CR period. But these are getting rarer. And as I found, after living in the region for two years in the mid 1990s, people simply don't want to talk about that period. They want to look ahead, to the glorious future that is being created, hour by hour, day by day.

Now and then glimpses of the resentment and damage that was done then are manifested in flare-ups during drinking sessions in which relatives who were killed are referred to and angry denunciations of the central government and its treatment of the area are uttered in unguarded moments. And even to this day, the strange semi-messianic rumours of an underground party (I heard this from a contact in Beijing, who had heard about it while in Europe) with arms, leaders and resources – all slowly working towards the final independence of Inner Mongolia. And all that provokes the awful thought that perhaps, after all, the so-called Inner Mongolia People's Party savagely attacked in the 1960s, and then declared to have been a figment of the imagination, did exist in some shape or form. Thus does the great Hall of Mirrors we call the CR continue to confuse and mystify.

What the CR Means Now, and for the Future

The CR, in fact, offers some very uncomfortable messages to anyone who cares to think about the PRC today. The genuine anger and social tensions it provoked question the laboriously manufactured 'unity' of the Chinese nation, especially along the sensitive national minority axis. Have these really gone away, especially in view of the increasing balkanization of Chinese society, with the haves, the getting theirs, and then the huge ocean of have nothings who are always just out of sight anywhere one goes? What if a similar opportunity to vent social rage on each other occurred again? Would the civil and social links in Chinese society be strong enough to make people look beyond these tensions to some greater notion of society that they belong to?

In fact, according to Ba Jin, and others who have commented on the so-called mysterious phenomenon of the CR, there is a sense in which it offered some profoundly unsettling insights into Chinese society, and its vulnerability. What was the social glue that held together such a loose mismatch of communities, and people, in the 1960s and 1970s – a naïve and overwhelming commitment to Utopian Maoism, and a hero-worship of one individual? For such a complex society, adherence to surprisingly simple ideals still holds true today. Money and material wealth have now replaced ideology, but the fervour remains the same. A Chinese teacher of mine several years ago commented that if the Chinese need one thing, it is an object of worship – and if that force of unification disappears, then chaos descends.

Whether the great mass-act of amnesia can be maintained about the CR, or about other 'sensitive' events in the narrative of Chinese history (like the 4 June 1989 Incident/Massacre) remains to be seen. Sentimentality can control some of the historical demons, for which witness the 'cute' CR restaurants that crop up from time to time in Chinese cities, and the occasional return of CR nostalgia. But at the moment the Ba Jin idea of a 'CR museum' remains a far-flung dream. Such a museum would be a true tour round the dark side of the Maoist dream. It would be a chance to look at what the Taiwanese writer Bo Yang called 'the ugly Chinaman syndrome' – a view of the real malice and latent dislike harboured by certain sections of Chinese society for others that is still prevalent today.[14] Even in the early 2000s, one of the common jokes at the British Embassy in Beijing when I worked there was that part of our diplomatic function was to carry messages from one warring Chinese ministry to another. This reached the dizzying unreality once of being begged by one ministry to tell another to back off – a message because of the labyrinth of Chinese face, that a foreigner might at least be able to convey with neutrality, but a local couldn't.

---

14 Bo Yang et al, *The Ugly Chinaman*, London 1993.

The bottom line is that the CR dragged one of the great hidden beasts of the Chinese underworld into the light of day – a form of social cannibalism. One of the great declarations of the New Chinese history after 1949 was that it had replaced the old 'dog eat dog' society with an equal, unified society. But in fact, the unwieldy juggernaut of the PRC is always veering from one side of the road it travels along to another, with frequent crashes and pile-ups. The Maoist incitement in the 1960s meant that, before too long, the only thing holding society together was the military force of the army – a return, no doubt pleasingly to Mao, of the principal of power coming from the barrel of a gun. The final court of appeal was therefore sheer physical force and brutality. And that has been the trump card of the Party whenever things have got dodgy since. But in the twenty-first century, with all the forces of globalization, and the commitment of so many other countries in the PRC's commercial and cultural life, it is hard to think that this sort of card could be easily played again. The impact would reverberate far beyond the PRC's shores, causing stock markets to tremble, perhaps crash, trade flows to convulse (imagine Wal-Mart needing to search elsewhere for the cheap goods with which it fills its US stores, increasing the buying power of citizens whose jobs were downsized or replaced by the very outsourcing that has manufactured the products they are buying). The Chinese cliché of holding a tiger by the tail and never being able to let go describes the predicament of the current government, which needs to take the path of compromise far more than its predecessors to whom brute force was always the final option, and frequently used.

So the CR helps to understand how the PRC got where it is now, and it sheds some light on the delicate fault lines of the new Chinese state. It also shows something about how history is relevant in the new gleaming China being built day by day. The CR belongs to the murky foundations, or the cracks between the bricks in the new walls being built – or the rickety building left behind in the great wave of development, just out of sight. Joyce complained, through the character of Stephen Dedalus in *Ulysses* that history was a nightmare he was trying to escape from. For many of the most energized, impressive entrepreneurs, the builders of the new PRC, that is doubly true. They are fleeing away from a history in which many of them were victimized, imprisoned and maltreated. Others are hiding up a history in which they committed what would now be considered criminal acts but in the topsy-turvy world of the CR were considered legitimate acts of revolutionary combat. Such a history runs deep, and so far silent under the new Chinese world. But there is always the lingering fear, perhaps even suspicion, that once the pedal is taken off the accelerator of 'unity', the new

CR might be far deadlier than the last, pitching classes against each other in a final free-for-all. And the only way to avoid that happening is to make sure, as quickly as possible, and at whatever cost, that as many people are crammed into the segment of society that has more to lose than gain if the current status quo crumbles. And, as I will show later on in this book, they are looked after by the new creed – economism, and trade-expansion.

CHAPTER FIVE:
THE DARK SIDE OF THE NEW PRC

The Canadian lawyer I met from time to time in Beijing always came out with the same odd statement. He did 'business', he said, only the business he did was the stuff 'above the table'. Then he leant across to me, over whatever we were eating, lowered his voice like he was letting me into a massive secret, and told me 'And my partner, Old Wang, who you have met – he does stuff under the table. Over in the dark side of the new China'.

I didn't really understand what someone like Old Wang, a man whose eyes were always blinking quickly, and who ran a consultancy service in Beijing did, until I read a book on business life in the PRC. There it was, set out in the chapter on how to deal with pay-offs and under the counter 'inducements' to officials and other interested parties on the journey towards wealth and riches in the PRC. The big multinationals, like BP and Shell, don't need to do this. They have the technology and the brand power to walk away if the other side doesn't do things their way. But for the smaller guys, at some point, the issue of whether or not to 'buy' businesses through pay-offs raises its head. This is the PRC, so nothing as unsophisticated as an out and out demand for pay-offs or kick-backs. Just an expectation, a suggestion hidden there between the lines, where, so often, real meaning is located.[1]

The more inventive deal with this problem by assisting people in getting their children to study abroad – though the currency of this has plummeted a bit over the last few years as the PRC has been hit by a glut of returning students with few jobs for them to do. Others used to be satiated by a nice trip abroad, and some generously funded shopping. But for the real big stuff these days, the 'red envelope' is de rigueur. Who can blame officials for this – still paid miniscule amounts even when they are in charge of massive budgets? The best example I heard of this was a mayor of a city in the south whose daughter was refused a visa to a European country because she had

---

1   James MacGregor, *One Billion Customers,* New York, 2005.

somehow, despite her father's 200–300 dollars wage a month, acquired over 1.5 million dollars in her bank account. And someone like Mr Wang is the guy that gets the 10 per cent in the contract for 'consultancy' services, money he disburses as he sees fit. If the US Military could get away with the 'don't ask, don't tell' principle when they wrestled with how to allow gays to serve in the army under the Clinton presidency, then why can't this method also help western business people preserve their principles, and at the same time satisfy the demands of their Chinese clientele? The dark side of the Chinese economy where these subterranean negotiations are undertaken is a fascinating place to wander into. It embraces the margins, the corners and hidden places of the new PRC– places where significant truths about the great project that is the PRC today can be found.

Where a Tour of the Dark Side Starts – Shenzhen, City of Sin and Sun

Such a tour of 'dark China' would begin in Shenzhen, a place where all history is bunk, chucked up in the last two and a half decades, where a local is someone who has survived there for more that a dozen years. Shenzhen is the ultimate expression of capitalist excess – all the more laudable for having a socialist sheen. The massive portrait of the 'architect' of the reform process, Deng Xiaoping, looks down on a city where so many buildings were chucked up so quickly in the mid 1980s that about 30 per cent of them fell down. Shenzhen, sunny and hot most of the year, is not a place where mercy lingers in the air. During the day, it is a heaving conglomeration of people, beggars, business people, cars and chaos. At night, the real mists arise and those brave enough to wander from their hotels will be greeted by voices, faces and hands extending from the darkness of the shadows, offering them 'beautiful women' for a few dollars – whispering to them that the satisfaction of their wildest dreams lies only a taxi drive away.

For a planned economy, the great reforms implemented in the 1980s after the devastation of the late Maoist period were pretty unplanned in their outcomes. The Party should be extended some sympathy here. They were left with a residue of chaos and damage probably unprecedented in modern history – a country that had been closed off, practicing self-destruction for over three decades. And, as long-term Beijing based journalist James Kynge points out, a country that was effectively bankrupt.[2] There was no option but to set in train changes that were likely to have unforeseen outcomes.

---

2 'China Shakes the World: The Rise of a Hungry Nation, London, 2006.

But the more predictable outcome was that while some would win in the new PRC and many would be lifted out of the poverty trap, many more would be left behind or abandoned. And over the years it has become clear that a lot of the biggest losers would be those who until then had been the glorious vanguard of the revolution, the peasants. For these, the best option was to flock towards the cities, constituting the biggest process of urbanization the world has ever seen. With the effective abandonment of internal control mechanisms in the late 1990s, people were set free from their work units and told to stand on their own two feet, at liberty to make money where they could.

The 'floating' population has had a massive impact on the PRC. At any one time in Beijing, the real population is probably 3 or 4 million more than the official figures through the hordes of temporary workers who go there to make their fortune. Needless to say, the success rate is not good. For men, there is the option of working on building sites, and hoping their bodies survive while they make enough money to call it a day. For women there are restaurants, where they can wait for a few yuan an hour – or 'barber shops' where they offer 'massages' – which eventually equates to prostitution. Prostitution is a boom industry in contemporary PRC.

So those taxis will take you to the beating heart of the dark side of the PRC – the 'entertainment' places and massage parlours where people can be bought and sold in the great human stock market. In this side of modern PRC, everything and everyone has their price. Souls are nothing more than the basic stock, up one day, down the other – commodified, packaged, abandoned and bought.

Zhuhai – Garden City

Beyond the fences and barriers that once separated Shenzhen from the rest of the PRC (or vice versa) capturing what Deng Xiaoping called 'the flies [of Western capitalist excess] that come in when the window [of reform] is opened' the road leads along the coast to Zhuhai. Zhuhai is another place erected overnight, with wide, landscaped highways, running from the gleaming new airport. The airport is one of the greatest white elephants of the modern world, built from corrupt money linked to the family of the former premier Li Peng, receiving only a few planes each day. The more sensible going to nearby Macau, or Hong Kong where there are airports that resemble a bit more closely the generally accepted idea of an international airport.The airport in fact is a good metaphor for Zhuhai, gleaming new, empty and pervaded by the ubiquitous smell of the modern

PRC, capturing an unmistakable, unique mixture of lethargy and cement. Going the 60 odd kilometres into town, that smell occurs again. In the day, Zhuhai is the retirement home of the favoured and privileged, surrounded by golf courses, reputedly the place of choice for rich Hong Kongese to accommodate their mistresses. That slightly dodgy air of privilege and unaccountability lingers under the trees along the roads, in the centre of the city. Everyone here is an outsider. During big events, the floating population that service the whims of the privileged are bussed out of the city, a kind of population cleansing. But they always return, for they are the lifeblood of this place which has such a tangibly impermanent feel about it.

Getting into evening, the plush hotels start to be invaded by the night world. Wandering out in the streets, by restaurants and shops, visitors (and in Zhuhai, in a sense, everyone is a visitor) will be approached by women in tight dresses, speaking a smattering of English, offering comfort and various types of massage. One of the more dissolute business people I had to deal with when I visited Zhuhai once, though, pointed out to me the true heart of darkness in Zhuhai's centre – the nightclubs and entertainment centres, within or around hotels, where menus of the hostesses are offered with a list of prices for each service. This is where the countrywomen come, in the hotels no doubt erected by their hometown's menfolk.

And what a sight the nightclubs are. Enter in, blink in the darkness, acclimatize your eyes, get led gently to your table in the outer edges of the dance room, and order a beer, from the scantily clad, friendly waitress, who then sits beside you and asks you, What more would you like? Then you realize, the place is full of women, only women, sitting, waiting and watching, in groups, all around the dance floor. A door opens to what looks like a side room, and you catch a glimpse of a row of smiling, leering, red male faces, in a darkened room, with the karaoke TV set in the centre throwing an unearthly blue light over the small audience, the men with their arms draped over the women, someone belting out yesteryear's most popular tune. This is where the night begins.

Three or four years ago Zhuhai hit the news. A delegation of Japanese had taken over a whole hotel, and had indulged in a three day orgy, causing outrage in the Chinese press at this further humiliation at the hands of the Japanese. But it wasn't surprising. Zhuhai offers nothing else except seafood and cheap sex. Macau is too expensive, and in any case, the real business there is gambling. Hong Kong has the Wanchai Red Light District which still pulls the punters in. But for the budget traveller, or the mainland businessman, Zhuhai is the place to go. Those that ask the hostess in the bar whether customers can just drink, will receive baffled looks and be asked whether what they are really wanting is two or three of the best, for a discount, and see how that sets up the night.

Journey to the West

Chinese nightclubs are a cultural phenomenon, with a unique drama, poetry and dark artistry all of their own. The road from Zhuhai up into the Western region, the poorer hinterland, takes one into a labyrinth, a world within a world. Take Lanzhou, one of the poorest regions, way over in the north- west between Xinjiang and Inner Mongolia. There they do an amazing party piece – nightclub fare with a difference. A floor show, of Freudian outlandishness, where, at the beginning rather than at the end, a fat lady waddles on and belts out a piece of Beijing opera with agonizing acoustics. Then it's the chance for some democracy – a couple of members of the audience walk up and, utterly unselfconsciously, sing some tunes. Then there is dancing – usually to a vaguely recognized disco tune from a decade or so ago. And then there are a couple of solo songs – a man in a black tuxedo, bawling out a piece of Italian opera (what else?), and finally a big song and dance event. My favourite among these was a piece where men dressed as doctors with white coats and stethoscopes waltzed around women made up as pregnant mothers, pillows stuffed under their sequined dresses.

What a thing the Chinese nightclub in the provinces is. Not overtly sexy, but with a whole semiotics of what is construed as desirable in the contemporary PRC. The women in tight dresses and high heeled black shoes and men in leather, but ever so tightly done up. And in the shadows around the edge of the dance floor is the real action. A sort of steady murmuring of bartering, where 'hostesses' move from table to table, ingratiating themselves with the patrons there, seeing what might be wanted – and then, as the evening wears on, peeling off with the customers they find, discreetly disappearing into the lobby and the world of rooms above, to do what they need to do, for an hour or two into the night.

Desire is the great unmentionable. There are raunchier places. Take Beijing, oddly a more unbridled place than that great harlot of the east, Shanghai, which seems to suffer sporadic moral panics, and ushers down one of the many 'strike hard' campaigns into local joy spots. During one of these in 2001, almost all the bars and entertainment places in the city were closed down, leaving the foreigners passing through (particularly the businessmen) looking like stranded fish out of water. But the real clubs for action are elitist affairs. There women or men can order what takes their fancy. Be pampered, massaged, pummelled until their bodies are aflame and then finished off by one, two or three of the servants who are there just for them (male prostitutes in China go under the disarming name of 'ducks'). Such a palace of pleasure was run by Lai Chaixing, the Fujianese Mr Fixit, famously abstemious on himself, but ever ready to look after the whims of officials and business people of use to him, housing them in his innocuous looking 'offices' which, when busted in 2000 after his massive smuggling racket was blown open, looked remarkably like a high class brothel.[3]

The nightclub worlds are as good a metaphor for the economic life of the current PRC. There is no sentiment here. Transactions are hard headed, based on who gets what from whom. Everything and everyone has a price tag. Where do the servants of this new China come from? Some are from the south and some from deep across in the west. Everyone is looking for a selling point. In what Uradyn Bulag has called, the eroticization of ethnic minorities, you can find Uiguer women in Xinjiang offered as a particular local 'delicacy'. Ditto the Mongolians in Inner Mongolia. But as a taxi driver told me bluntly once, local woman aren't considered much of a premium. Russians, blond haired, blue eyed, they would set punters back three, four times what the locals would. 'I had a Russian once' the taxi driver declared airily. 'OK, but the thing about Russians is the minute they have kids they get old and ugly.'

Moral Panic

It is a common complaint. Chinese themselves complain about the selfishness and lack of trust that has corroded the old values in their society. In every interaction, people are looking at you trying to work out just what use you are going to be to them, they complain. There is little sense of a larger society (thus the general lack of indigenous charities in Chinese society) or of a civic world that needs nurturing and preserving, something development agencies have been noting for years. People's first commitment is to themselves, then to their families and only after all of that do they leave a small residue for their locality and then their country. Trust between individuals or groups is scarce. People seek in their previous lives, or in their backgrounds, demonstrable grounds to trust others. The history of denunciations and campaigns rooting out people over the last half-century has not helped.

---

3   This case is dealt with in some detail in MacGregor's book, cited above.

All of the normal registers of social tension are increasing. Divorces are up, rates of sexually transmitted diseases are going through the roof (long gone are the days in the early 1990s when AIDS was talked of specifically as a foreigner's disease). Prostitution, gambling and drug taking are thriving. It's hard to work out what crime statistics are reliable– but from being a reasonably safe society, the PRC has become as prone to waves of robberies, rapes and murders as any other – all this compounded by the general reluctance of authorities to admit these problems exist at all and then to greatly under-report the crimes. The violence visited by the state on citizens is another blind spot. It used to be that the state had a monopoly on this, something it from time to time outsourced (like during the CR). The state had the power of life and death over individuals, and could perform whatever indignities it liked on them. The agents of the state (police, public security bureau personnel, army) were able to practice any level of thuggery, even torture leading to death.

In the era of privatization, there is now a thriving private sector of criminals, thugs and pimps, who have taken over these functions and act with similar levels of impunity. Newspapers report, more than they ever did before though still with some diffidence, the daily cases of local strongmen doing over any one standing in their way. This ranges from stubborn peasants who are refusing to move from their land for construction projects, to aggrieved common citizens who have been conned or had over by some scam. For these people, the judicial system is frequently a joke, with judges and prosecutors easily paid off or influenced by their political masters. The honourable exceptions are all the more glaring for their rarity. At the end of the day, hefty bribes will help anyone get off.

The reform process has helped bring into being over the last two decades a world where breakneck galloping for growth at the cost of everything else (including the environment, social equality, ideology) has left people dizzy and disorientated. Imagine that you are a 45-year-old Chinese. In your life you have seen, first the extreme, puritanical egalitarianism of the CR. You have seen cast iron, ideological certainly, emanating from the great figure of Mao. The structure of your daily life was arranged around Mao – reading his works, studying editorials from the *People's Daily*, working together in work units or communes, needing to get permission for the tiniest detail of your life, from who and when you could marry, to where you can work, how long, what position and what you do.

Then, in the space not of a generation or two, but in only a few years, the whole of this is blown away. Maoism is never overtly disowned, but everybody knows that Maoism à la CR is dead in the water, and that

Marxism-Leninism, the formal ideological basis for the Party, is something to relegate to formal party meetings, while 99.9 per cent of real life goes on outside, like Church on Sunday for the small percentage of active faithful in the West. There is nothing to replace this except rampant capitalism. The real God in the new society is money. You are what you earn. What that means for those that earn nothing is that they suddenly become invisible.

In this new world, the moral strictures, the traditions, the framework of the old life is gone. For those with money, there is power, and with power, almost unlimited licence to do as they please. Marriage to many becomes a tired cliché, cadres spending hours each evening in nightclubs of varying degrees of sleaziness where sex is only a few yuan away. The sporadic 'clamp downs' are the exceptions that prove the rule, public displays of carefully managed, hollow indignation that are viewed with general cynical amusement by the public and by the targets. Like the immense trade in pirated or counterfeit goods (of which the PRC produces 70 per cent of the world's stock) the problem is so endemic and immense that it is almost insoluble.

For this 'post Maoist type man', the pronouncements of the Party are viewed with weary, but compliant obedience. The deal is that there is a ring-fenced area. One Party rule, for instance, and all out attacks on the Party and its pantheon of saints are off-limits. But everything else is up for grabs. An entrepreneur in Xian who I talked to in 2005 told me the bottom line, 'When you deal with Party officials, it is simple. You make it seem like all your great ideas are theirs. You treat them well, look after them, and they leave you alone. 'How do you look after them?', I naively asked. He raised his eyebrows. It hardly needed saying.

The Post Maoist Type Man

The erosion of public trust has meant that even more value is placed on '*guangxi*' or connections – the need to have introductions and links to people, either through school, home, university, or something else, which are seen as reliable and proven. Simply linking up with others without some intermediary is unheard of. To most Chinese, when they talk about their society, it comes across as something like seventeenth century British philosopher Hobbes's 'natural state of man' – a social jungle, full of predators, villains and cheats, where 'man eats man', and no one can be trusted.

The fall away from utter certainty to complete lack of ideological commitment is violent and sudden for Post Maoist type men, and has left a palpable sense of disorientation and unease in contemporary Chinese society. For people of all generations, in the end, the great communist project has failed to deliver. Most have a sense that the current status quo, of breakneck development, whatever the environmental or social costs, while it may be the easiest route, is not a sustainable one. The divisions in society mean that we return to the problem of the second chapter – many Chinas rather than one.

The Post Maoist type man has the consolation of owning his own house, having one, or several cars, in which he can hurtle around the ring roads of the major cities and scuttle into his private exclusive clubs. He can travel anywhere he wants, he likes buying Rolexes, spending enormous amounts of money on meals and playing golf in the courses that lie on the outskirts of most Chinese cities or towns. He may have a wife, but he will most of the time have other lovers, who he can pay off when he gets tired, or simply employ from time to time. In such a world, social bonds are flexible and easy. Such a man, however, despite his wealth and success cannot vote for the political party he likes, nor express certain opinions about his own country. And he cannot ever own the land on which his investments and houses are built (that is all government owned – the one trump card the Party still has). He can easily attract the unwelcome attention of a Machiavellian bureaucracy that can suddenly, capriciously, hone in on his tax situation, or his employees, or his investments, and extract evidence of myriad illegalities that can see him sent away for several years. The PRC's second richest man, Yang Bing, was felled in 2002 for a combination of becoming too involved in North Korea and for reported tax crimes. The first few Fortune 100 lists of China's richest produced in the late 1990s and early 2000s were jokingly called 'The Death Lists' by some commentators because appearing on them meant attracting the scrutiny of the authorities who could then crawl through people's affairs and suddenly produce a crime for which they could be banged up indefinitely.

In any country, experience of the legal system is unsettling and often unpredictable. But in the PRC, the pain one can suffer at the hands of the police, the courts and the Party that hovers behind them, can be never-ending. Judgements can be perverse, politically motivated and near impossible to reverse or appeal against. Almost anything can be elevated to a crime. In this Kafkaesque world (and in many ways Kafka rather than Orwell was a far more accurate describer of the worlds of both Communism and Post Communist societies), the process of judgement and retribution can take forever and never make sense.

So for the Post Maoist type man, it is easy to see why there is a slight queasiness, a sense that the main thing is to live for the moment, along with a constant and assiduous attempt to have a bolt hole, a hideaway, in case things go wrong. Thus the rumours some years back of the huge volume of foreign currency that swept out of the country, feathering the nest of successful but nervy big wigs and entrepreneurs. Thus also the popularity of acquiring passports and travel documents for western countries, even when everything was hunky-dory in the PRC, so that there was an exit route just in case things went badly wrong. Not to say that there wasn't enormous fun for the Post Maoist type man. But it seemed that for the really successful ones, the multimillionaires and top entrepreneurs, there was a gradually acquired asceticism, and the famous Li Kaisheng of Hong Kong's practice of adage that the really wealthy got there by being mean to themselves and generous to others.

And such a creeping sense of nihilism and disaffection manifested itself further in society in the popularity of superstitious belief systems like the Falungong. Over the last two decades, Christian missionaries from the West have found the PRC a rich picking ground for proselytizing. There seems to be thirst for meaning after the big truths of the 1960s and 1970s went down in flames. There are reportedly almost 100 million practicing Christians in the PRC today.

For the children of the Post Maoist men, modern PRC is a paradox. They have never had it so good, and are as awash with opportunities and material goods as their western counterparts. The one child policy so rigorously implemented since the early 1980s means the old days of seven or more in a family sharing next to nothing are gone. Children are the recipients of the love and attention of extended families, giving rise to the very modern phenomenon of little emperors and empresses – kids who are nurtured from the day they are born and for whom expense is nothing. London is now full of such children, coughing up tuition fees that would make most British blink, buying cars locally, sometimes apartments and starting to do business here. But whether these children have much affection for the PRC, beyond a defensive nationalism when abroad, is another matter. For them, the name of the game is making loads of money. And then, after they have done that, they will start wrestling with the same issues of meaning, satisfaction, contentment that seem to have poleaxed the western societies that they have been emulating for so long. And as for them, they are now starting to find the great paradoxes of western society that are being imported into their own – the problems of confusion, dislocation, instability and senses of insecurity that traditional societies simply didn't seem to have much time for.

In fact, in the next two decades, the PRC will become more and more like our societies – and less and less Chinese. This is another point of attack on the notion of what it is to be Chinese in a global, postmodernist world. The deal in the last two decades has been that economic development has to deliver everything – and that political and other areas of life need to stay stagnant while this great area is attended to. But that deal, surely, is time limited. What will the increasingly large, affluent Chinese middle class want in the next two decades? This will dictate how the PRC develops and what sort of place it looks like in 2026. One thing is for certain. The solid, restricted sense of placing one set of activities into one area (moneymaking and commercial) and one into another (intellectual and political) is riven with problems. And don't be surprised if the form of 'Chinese democracy' that comes from this process at the end might look nothing like democracy we have seen or experienced before. After all, Chinese politics, as I will describe it in the next chapter, is quite simply a law unto its own.

CHAPTER SIX:
GETTING USED TO UNDERSTANDING
MODERN CHINESE DOUBLESPEAK

Simon Leys, the great sinologist, was among the first to point out, in the early 1970s, that there seemed to be two languages in modern PRC. An 'official language', used by cadres and party apparatchiks, which was shrill and hectoring, full of exaggeration and hyperbole – and a natural street language, used by people in daily discourse.

The CR period was the acme of politicized language. Terms and phrases from that period have merited dictionaries of their own like, 'Cow Ghosts and Snake Spirits. Capitalist Roaders. Imperialist paper tigers'. The general intensity and level of invective became a physical assault in its own right. This should not be surprising. The PRC, like many preceding dynasties, is a highly discursive political environment. Words matter. That great demagogue of the CR period, Mao Zedong's wife, Jiang Qing, declared famously that in the current battle, words and not objects were weapons. Even in a movement that involved intense levels of physical violence, language made its own contribution, and created an extra level of violence. Words classifying victims were plastered across boards and hung from their necks. They were daubed in slogans upon the landscape. Taboo terms were publicly used – the most fearsome expletives and innuendos. In public struggle sessions, victims were hauled up and abandoned to tirades of, sometimes formulaic, sometimes customized, attack. To this day connoisseurs can date particular language structures to the CR period fairly accurately. It was one of those historical movements that created its own modes of saying.

Doing Things with Words in Chinese Politics

Language is important in China, because of all the unifying features in this enormous, constructed 'imagined community' (slightly adapting historian Benedict Anderson's term for the mental bonds uniting disparate communities), the written language is one of the strongest. Cantonese, with its eight tones and its specific vocabularies and standard Mandarin seem as different as German and English. Shanghainese and Sichuanese 'dialects' sometimes sound like languages from different continents. But the one thing underpinning all of these is the unity of the written language – despite the modifications made since the 1950s in simplifying some of the characters from their traditional forms. That at least seems firm empirical evidence to point to a unity in other areas – culture, for instance, or society. One could argue that a similar unity is supplied by the Roman alphabet in Europe, but there are very different word orders and grammars between the languages in this area – in the PRC, on the whole, a written piece is as comprehensible in Hainan way down in the south as it is in Helongjiang, thousands of kilometres to the north. The Chinese written language is undeniably one of the greatest achievements of human communication.

The development of Chinese writing has been a fascinating one. In the past, the complexity of the written language restricted literacy to only the absolute elite – those with the leisure and time to be able to master the thousands of characters needed for communication. The mandarinates based their power simply on this access to literacy. There was a movement of '*bai hua*', colloquializing written Chinese in literature, which started around the time of the great Chinese novel *Dream of the Red Chambers* in the late eighteenth century, and continued to the 4 May Movement in 1919, a student rebellion during the Republic of China period that voiced opposition to what was seen as the unequal and bad settlement forced on China at the end of World War I. The attempt to disseminate and spread literacy further continued throughout the 1930s, with contributions by intellectuals like the Taiwan based Hu Shi, and the man widely regarded as the greatest of all modern Chinese writers, Lu Xun.

The communists, when they came to power in 1949 were to be the most energetic promoters of full literacy, spearheading campaigns to increase character recognition in the countryside and increasing the numbers of people attending at least primary education. But one of their main tools was the process of simplifying written characters, something that had been the brainchild of people like Hu Shi and others, who realized that the sometimes intensely complicated characters that had existed for centuries (sometimes even thousands of years) before were impractical for most people to learn. With their usual genius for organization and institutionalization, the communists set up a committee that approved the reduction of stroke numbers for a raft of characters, often by simplifying both the radical for a character, and the strokes in its main body. A typical example is the Chinese for 'to let', *ran*, which was reduced from over a dozen strokes to simply four. The result of this is that China is now one of the most literate societies in the world.

How the communists affected the modes of expression within the Chinese language, though, was more sophisticated. What is incontrovertible is that they imported a raft of concepts and terms that changed the way Chinese could think about social and political issues. While frequently credited to Mao Zedong, in fact this process of 'sinicizing' Marxism-Leninism into Chinese was the collective effort of a number of intellectuals and political figures from the 1920s onwards, of whom Mao was only one of the more minor members. Chen Duxia, for instance, was particularly important in writing about Marx's main theories. In the great rewriting of history after 1949, this was often conveniently overlooked, or simply denied.

Mao's main contribution was simply to relate Marxist theories to the concrete situation in China. Mao was not a particularly profound social thinker, but he was certainly shrewd and clever in taking the theories that were useful to him, and presenting them in his own works. The result was a new way of speaking – the introduction, to take one simple but obvious example, of class terms into Chinese, by which to categorize people (proletariat, bourgeoisie). This was accompanied by descriptions of certain phases of history (feudalism), and the raft of terms to support this renarrativization. More ambitiously, Mao also prescribed strict parameters for imaginative works – canonizing socialist realism, and the adherence to everyday life in fictional works, portraying the struggles and victories of the common people.

Such 'linguistic engineering', as it has been called (discourse management is another term) could be likened to the process of thought control described by George Orwell in his dystopic vision of the communist present/future in *1984*. In fact, while Orwell may have addressed the manipulations achieved by the uses of specific kinds of language in his journalism, 'newspeak' seems only ever to have been intended as a satire on political language rather than an attempt to describe the real thing. There has always been a disjuncture between political language in the PRC, and the 'street language' that Simon Leys noted in the early 1970s. The period of greatest management, the CR, saw a plethora of Red Guard pamphlets and pronouncements that, highly paradoxically, vented far more opinions and thoughts, in a more varied register and tone, than before or since. But it is true that the promotion of a certain 'official' way of speaking was one means amongst many for the political centre in Beijing to pursue its project of centralization. At least, there was a common formal political language spoken throughout the PRC – even if the people speaking it were doing so in dialects that were barely comprehensible to each other.

The general result of the use of this highly exaggerated, didactic language was that, as soon as the political swells underpinning it passed by, and new campaigns started, such striking forceful language was left stranded. The most glaring example of this was the hyperbole poured down on the head of Mao's 'chosen successor', Lin Biao, in the late 1960s, a period during which he was lauded as Mao's comrade in arms, his most precious companion and the true heir to his mantle. All of this looked decidedly odd when he was being vehemently denounced as a traitor and scab in 1972 when the news of his fleeing the PRC and dying in a plane crash over Outer Mongolia in late 1971 was made public. Such extreme about-turns nurtured a sense of weary cynicism in the Chinese that has persisted to this day.

Heard it All Before: Cynicism and Contemporary Chinese Language

Cynicism about formal political language in contemporary PRC is at crisis levels. This is not to say that in most other countries pronouncements about or by politicians are not taken with a large dose of salt. But on the whole, the sheer distance between the way that politicians speak in the PRC and the language used by everyone else is particularly glaring. While discourse analysts like Normal Fairclough have argued, in his book *New Labour, New Language*, that the whole drift of 'post modern' societies had been for politicians to adopt language that seemed everyday to make them seem close to people (thus Tony Blair's cringingly awful adoption of his attempt at the 'man in the street' tone when he appears on shows like 'Richard and Judy'), in the PRC, distance is still required. Politicians, on the whole, live in their unelected zone, confined to compounds, the most auspicious of which is Zhongnanhai in Beijing, but which is replicated in the walled in, carefully guarded compounds throughout other provincial cities in the PRC. If anything serves as a good symbol of the continuing distance between those ruled, and those ruling, then these geographical zones stand out. High-level cadres continue to exist in a world of chauffeur driven cars, carefully managed timetables and general distance and exclusion from the great masses of the people. This is compounded by the language they use, exemplified in the formal speeches they are fond of making at events like the welcoming of delegations, or the stage-handled congresses that are held from time to time.

In the last ten years, perhaps only former premier, Zhu Rongji adopted anything like a 'personal style' but then he was branded on his so-called 'plain speaking' character, and already had considerable political capital from his past as a condemned rightist in the 1950s, and an astute economic manager of Shanghai in the 1980s and 1990s. The public tone of most Chinese politicians remains drearily unvaried – a fondness for empty hyperbole, for formulaic structures in their language and a general reluctance to adopt anything that might sound idiosyncratic or personal. Cadres along the length and breadth of the PRC are all adept at making eloquent speeches about the particular progress and economic glories of the PRC now – all of it in a sort of single style speech that might be called 'borrowed language', belonging, it seems, to a common reservoir of expressions, metaphors or phrases that need to be used on only these occasions and in these contexts.

Veterans of the public circuit in the PRC – outsiders like foreign business people or diplomats or, from time to time, academics (more of these later) will know the scenario well. In the PRC, nothing can be said to exist before the baptism of a public meeting of some sort. They range from the massive, flower bedecked, journalist laden congresses held in the Great Hall of the People in Beijing every year, to the small daily gatherings that still go on in what are left of the work units or teaching institutions. Here the East indeed meets the West. In the beginning was the word – or rather, lots of words, in pretty similar orders, sounding the same, saying the same thing, and, the more they are listened to, saying nothing. Opening up a company? Then that needs an inaugural meeting, with women dressed in Qipaos holding red ribbons, scissors and flowers, for the visiting dignitaries to cut. Need to welcome a delegation just off the plane from the other side of the world? What better than a welcoming forum, with red banners stuck against the back of the wall, and half-hour long speeches, proclaiming the eternal and undying friendship between the PRC and the peoples of the whole world.

The standard speech in the PRC in 2006 runs along very predictable lines. It will begin with warm words of welcome, then it will set out the recent amazing economic successes and the work that the Party and the country have done to achieve this. It will throw in a few popular phrases from the time – that will be the one area of occasional change and difference. And then it will chuck out a list of statistics, years and growth rates – all of which could be true, or false. It's hard to tell! And then the final rousing wind up – for a 'more prosperous, more successful, more this, more that two thousand and whatever'.

Slogans are an area of real interest, as are the various speech acts that Chinese officials use at these events. For such a highly organized political culture, it is no surprise that as each campaign came and went, so did a whole new set of slogans, each one leaving a residue in the linguistic collective memory. In the 1950s, in the great initial leap towards economic industrialization (something that, interestingly, prefigured the next such rush in the 1980s), it was all about 'push forward', 'grasp', 'vehemently implement', 'vigorously construct'. But then in the 1960s, politics was put back in command, after the costs of such reckless developments extended to ruined harvests, economic depletion and millions of deaths. In the CR people ceased speaking to each other courteously. They peppered their speech with language which had migrated in from the slogans produced at the time, heavy with verbs like 'smash' (as in the phrase 'Smash the Four olds'), 'root out', 'dig,' and 'hit'. The world was full of hidden enemies, who were concealed even between the lines of speeches and words. A cadre one week would denounce and in the next find his very words of denunciation turned against him. Such an environment bred high levels of insecurity – but somehow, the production of slogans carried on, deep into the 1970s, when, in a period of exhaustion, people were simply invoked, though one of the cryptic utterances came from Chairman Mao, to 'dig deep' and store grain. The more positive environment of the 1980s meant that there was a return to 'pushing forward', 'building' and 'constructing'. The nasty hiccough of the Tiananmen Square Incident/Massacre in 1989 brought back the need to 'smash', 'dig up', and 'root out' again. A particularly brutal news programme from around that time contained the blood-curdling promise to 'look deep for the ugly face of the criminal leaders of the anti-party clique'. But, when the paramount leader/emperor/Chair of the Chinese Bridge Playing Association (his only formal role of responsibility, despite the enormous power he wielded) Deng Xiaoping decreed that China had no other choice but to continue on the path of 'opening up' and 'reforming' during his famous southern tour in 1991, the positive vocabulary returned.

Years have seasons, and they also have cycles of campaigns. When I lived in the PRC during 1994 and 1996, the great campaign was for 'patriotism' (*aiguozhuyi*), which, in one particularly bright middle school student I know, elicited the unconsciously wise response, 'but love which country'? In Inner Mongolia, the area where I was based, there was also the constant demanding of 'unity of all national minority groups' and, of course, declaring the ten thousand year rule of the Party. When *Falungong* came on the scene in 1998–9, suddenly there were slogans to stamp out superstition, and rely on science. The return of Hong Kong in 1997 provoked similar outpourings of retrospective backslapping – 'the successful handover of Hong Kong in 1997', along with the paradoxical notion of 'one country, two systems'. But in the noughties, economism has dominated language. Now it is all 'for a more prosperous, more successful, more developed' China. There are constant references to the 'twenty five years of reform and opening up'. Deng Xiaoping was the 'nucleus' of the second generation of China's leaders (and, of course, the Chief architect of the reforms), Jiang Zeming, his successor, that of the third. Now we have Hu Jintao as the nucleus of the fourth generation. The latest buzzword, as of Spring 2006, is for a 'harmonious' society, and the mildly puzzling assertion of a 'socialist' countryside.

Such self-descriptions seep into the language of those who talk about the PRC from outside. They are accepted as the terms for debate about what is happening in the PRC. The hunt is always on for new, emerging slogans. It used to be that people, in the pre 1980's period, could plot the rise and fall of political fortunes on where people were listed when they met foreign visitors or appeared at large meetings. Liu Shaoqi, Mao's tragic number two from 1949 to 1966, and the chief victim of the CR, was dead meat when his place in a list of Party leaders slipped from just after Mao to number seven, after Lin Biao, and Mao's wife. The long-standing premier, Zhou Enlai, wisely remained at number three throughout his long political career – Liu's successor, Lin Biao, was to meet a similarly sticky end. It seems, at least until the 1990s, far from four being the unlucky number in the PRC, two was.

Statistics and Lies

Because of the claim that the Party was promoting 'science' and because of the stress they put on 'scientific truths' being at the heart of their ideology, and of their practice of developing and improving the PRC, it is hardly surprising that much Chinese political, public discourse now seems densely empirical. Great swathes of statistics and figures are regurgitated. During my embassy period, the favourite one was to refer to Britain being the 'largest investor in the EU in the PRC' (this was seen as delivering brownie points for us over our main competitors, Germany and France, in currying favour of the Chinese, offsetting the perennial problems of our being seen as far too close to the Americans and intrinsically conservative). Anyone interrogating this statistic slammed into a number of walls. One was simply that the 'custodians' of this figure at the time, the Ministry of Foreign Trade and Economic Co-operation (MOFTEC, since replaced by the Ministry of Trade) were never able to produce a list of the so-called investments constituting this figure. Then it became clear that, as far as yearly investment went, the Germans were ahead of us. So we then simply said that the figure referred to 'cumulative investment' – the amount the UK had piled into the PRC in the last 40 years. But how much of that money had ever actually been received was another issue. There was contractual investment, and committed investment – that which was received, and that which was promised. For a fairly simple statistic, therefore, things didn't seem that straightforward.

But like it or not, most speeches now contain a good dose of simply stupefying statistics, setting out the billions of dollars of money flowing in, flowing out, going here and going there. Some analysts like Beijing-based Joe Studwell in *The China Dream*, a rather pessimistic puncturing of the popular idea that China is now at last economically standing up and about to make the rest of the world very, very rich, look at some of these claims about 'contracts signed' and investment flowing into the PRC. On one trip by a leading Chinese leader to the US, for instance, of the multi-billion pound contracts signed, literally none were ever carried forward. But the money went on the overall statistics, putting the PRC as the second largest attractor of foreign direct investment after the US. There is also the perennial problem of just what the basis for some of the fantastic figures delivered up by the provinces is. Some of them seem, on interrogation, to look suspiciously like the returns for crop yields put in by fearful Party officials during the most vicious period of the famines in the late 1950s and early 1960s, most of which were subsequently proved to have been entirely fabricated.[1]

In 2006, after the glut of figures, creating the impression of overwhelming activity, some of which was true, and some of which may not have been, though most of it was indistinguishable and indigestible by the listener, there was also a little space left in the typical public speech for a nod to the importance of the Party – and of ideology. Marxism-Leninism is still paid lip service, even after the final victory of blatant pragmatism. These parts of public speeches are received rather like the 'religious bits' in school assemblies, given hushed respectful silence, expected and endured. But they now sit a little oddly with the environment in which they are in, peppered with phrases like, 'Under the glorious guidance of the Party,' 'wise leadership,' 'with President Hu as the nucleus of the fourth generation'.

Out on the Chinese streets, in the world of informal speech, finding a sincere proponent of Marxism-Leninism is as rare these days as unearthing a mint Penny Black. And such traditionalists, when they are found, are usually as aware of their rarity as those that find them. On the whole, after the 'formal' speeches, at dinners and other events, officials will have an

---

1   Joe Studwell, *The China Dream: The Elusive Quest for the Last Great Untapped Market on Earth*, London, 2002.

ironic gleam in their eyes, and a slight smirk on their lips when quizzed over the ideological content of their speeches. While never as blatant or overt as saying that they don't believe a word of what they have just said, there will be undercurrents of self-mockery. The mouths will say one thing, the facial expressions something completely different.

Some of the world's greatest literature is in Chinese. People in the PRC with any level of education have a keen sense of this huge literary tradition, stretching back over three millennia. The great classics of Confucius, Mencius and the *Book of Changes*, through the poets of the Song and Tang dynasty and right up to the great sprawling narrative novels of the Ming (*Journey to the West*, otherwise known as *Monkey* and the perennial *Water Margin*, made famous in the West by the 1970s Japanese TV rendition). Someone once described Chinese as the language that God would speak – a grammar that has none of the irritations of tenses, genders, or nasty cases – with a beautiful, but expressive simplicity – and, of course, the aesthetic wonder of the word-signs, characters, in which so much more meaning can be conveyed in their writing than western or Cyrillic alphabets.

The more damaging effect of so many years of abuse and misuse of language, however, has been that, at least for the formal registers, hardly anyone either believes what is said, or, for that matter, cares. Great respect is accorded to the statements of officials, no matter how gnomic or abstruse, and a great industry has grown up of those who are able to offer their services 'interpreting' what is said and putting it into comprehensible 'street speech'. Of course, there are frequent conflicts between members in this expanding fraternity of 'interpreters'. The most striking phenomenon though is simply that there are still 'two languages' – the language used by politicians in the public arena, and then the language people use with each other. Such disjuncture reflects the fractures in Chinese society as a whole, between the rulers and the ruled, between those whose words need to be given face and listened to and those that are just 'normal.' One day, perhaps quite soon, a PRC politician might take the path of someone like Tony Blair and deliberately adopt a register almost competing with others to declare his normality and closeness to the people – no doubt this would create the same rich comedy of fervently declared sincere phoniness that Blair has become the greatest master of. But with the variations among the dialects, living levels and cultures of those who live within the PRC now, it is difficult to see how such a common, credible language might be forged. Until then, the golden rule needs to be applied. What people say is one thing. What they really mean is something else. And in fact, the last thing anyone using formal Chinese language would ever mean is what they are actually saying, a phenomenon that looks likely to continue into the future.

CHAPTER SEVEN:
HOW TO WIN FRIENDS AND INFLUENCE
PEOPLE IN THE PRC

There is one, and only one thing, that we can be certain about in the contemporary entity we call the PRC. And that is that power, notions of power, exercising of power and visible signs of power, are never far from the surface of the great lake of humanity and human behaviour that the PRC encompasses, and that those both outside, and who swim in its waters experience and see.

There is an archaeology of power, as French philosopher Michel Foucault pointed out. The social psychologist Michael Bond wrote in a very early study of the behaviour of the Chinese (in his book, most of his field work was based on Hong Kong Chinese) that the system of initiating, building and then maintaining relations in the Chinese social world, and how people were related to each other, was founded on the simple historical fact that in earlier dynasties resources were controlled by very few people.[1] The systems that prevailed throughout ancient Chinese states were largely oligarchies, straying into tyrannies, with power concentrated in the hands of a tiny number. The emperors of the dynasties that make up the great patchwork of Chinese history exercised utter domination. The world revolved around them, so that even the accidental sighting of them by 'commoners' was rewarded with execution.

Things have changed, but sometimes not much. In 1949, part of the great communist project was to dismantle this feudal history. It was a common objective then and now, to replace the system of man by that of law. But traditions of behaviour run deep, and Mao had a system of hero worship erected around him that must rank as the one of the most exhaustive and complete the world has ever seen – only, perhaps, exceeded by that of the North Koreans and their ongoing deification of Kim Il Sung.

---

1   Michael Harris Bond (ed), *The Psychology of the Chinese People*, Hong Kong, 1987.

Those excesses are in the past, but two general principles remain true. Few have power in the PRC and the most truly powerful are not the most obvious. Power, we can state here, is more like a kind of energy, a force field (to hark back to Foucault again). It is an influence, sometimes spoken, sometimes not. Those who are truly powerful in the PRC define the terms of discourse without even speaking. Mao, through his silence, sealed the fates of many of those who were around him and fell foul of the system. A word or two may have saved Liu Shaoqi, but Mao, by saying nothing, as good as condemned him to death. In contemporary PRC, the truly powerful have others to mouth their thoughts, to channel their ideas and to fill out their ideologies. Deng Xiaoping was a master of this. Holding no formal positions of power beyond, early on his non-executive 'rule' a vice premiership, he was to determine the general direction of the country for over two decades, even deep into his nineties when it was suspected that he was barely compos mentis most of the time.

Playing 'Spot the Leader' in the PRC

It is a good game, for those at any stage in their experience of the PRC. Go into a meeting room, full of faces opposite, or look around one of those great 'welcoming' events. Better still, be at a large formal dinner. And try and work out who is the person who has most clout. It's certainly not something one can reduce to a simple rule. One used to airily state that the Party Secretaries, either in work units, towns or provinces, were the real wielders of power. But these days where the division between private and public, Party and personal is a bit more complicated, that isn't always the case. Indeed, a Chinese lawyer in Beijing told me that in some places, the Party Secretaries have to seek the help of other intermediaries to sort problems out – a return to the days of the old warlords in the 1930s, where each area had its own strongman.

In so-called private companies, it is sometimes not enough to carry the name of President, Chief Executive, or even Chairman. The Party secretary may still have real clout. They can't be excluded. It might just be that someone who has some other form of influence, some son of a powerful cadre from the past, who still enjoys political capital from the brand of his or her name, can use this to trump other contending claims. More rarely it might be someone with specific technical knowledge. And sometimes, more intriguingly still, it might be the last person you expect, someone with some kind of 'position' in the great shadowy hinterland of the Chinese social landmass – some function, in the mammoth security services perhaps, which is known, but not fully explicated and means that they too have the aura of 'power' – all the more seductive and impressive for being subterranean.

So of the dozen faces looking at you across the table, just assuming that position and geography (the guy in the centre with the biggest name placard in front of him) will tell you who is the real force won't always be true. Scrutinizing people's job names on cards to see whose sounds the most important, or looking at their faces to see who looks the oldest – that won't finally tell either. The only way is to carefully watch how people speak, who is deferred to, what people's body language is, and who seems to speak and then be followed.

During my first prolonged stay in the PRC in the mid 1990s, I befriended a self-proclaimed dissident – one of the 'victims' of the CR, a survivor of sorts, who had learned impeccable spoken English from the BBC World Service (though oddly, his listening comprehension was terrible – but perhaps that was just because in any language he was a bad listener). He had a scar down his cheek, from, he claimed, being beaten up by Party activists as a result of his pursuing his claims for compensation at the end of the CR too aggressively. There was a wonderful ambiguity about his story and many vague and empty spots. But it was he, one cold afternoon, in his tiny hovel in the west of the city, who introduced me to the concept of '*suan*'. '*Suan*' literally means 'to reckon', 'to calculate'. But as he pointed out, when you talk of people whose words '*suan*', that literally means 'whose writ runs here – who has the final say'. 'Wherever you go,' he declared, 'you ask one question. Work unit, company, government – who's the guy here with the final say. Whose words are what carry weight? You talk to anyone else, and you're wasting your time. There'll be one, at most two, who you should track down. The rest, just give them a bye bye'.

He was right. Working at the embassy, most days were filled with plotting who was in, who was out, in the various labyrinthine government ministries, or the provinces. The real industry was looking for those who were being shifted up or down. For a while, there were signs that Premier Zhu Rongji was on his way out. Reports of his public appearances slipped down the playing order in the evening news. This was connected to his failure to do a deal over World Trade Organization (WTO) when everything seemed to be in place in 1999, largely because, when he visited the US that year, Clinton was somewhat distracted by his recent scandals and could not find any available capital that he had not squandered on himself to lobby for the deal in the Congress. Like anywhere, power in the PRC is all the more fascinating because of its vagaries. It comes and goes, suddenly disappears in one place only to reappear in another. To describe Chinese power though is no easy thing, simply because the system as a whole thrives on the lack of transparency. Opaqueness is as necessary for Chinese politicians as water to fish or air to mammals. The light of publicity would kill most of the ecosystem on which these creatures depend to live.

The History of Power in the PRC

It was an even more brutal game in the past. Over decades, Mao sniffed out and accrued power to himself, so that, by the late 1960s, almost all decisions of any significance needed to be referred to him. His treatment of those like General Peng Dehuai or President Liu Shaoqi who were construed as opposing him or carrying out activities against his wishes was brutal. Peng Dehuai had been one of the great heroes of China's epic battle against first the Japanese and then the Nationalists before 1949. Seemingly secure in his position in the 1950s, his famous criticisms of Mao's policies during the Great Leap Forward in 1957 and then the years of famine that followed were initially rewarded by him being removed from positions of responsibility and shipped off to his home province of Sichuan. But the Chinese system is not so forgiving, and to Mao and those around him, Peng was firstly a potential opponent and, secondly a nasty bellwether vane for other disaffected elements in the country and to the leadership of the Party during this period the enemy was all around.

The CR was the opportunity for Peng to be dealt with. He was brought back to Beijing, and struggled against throughout the summer of 1967, a year, which was, according to accounts, particularly hot. Peng, a former top ranking general, war hero, and politician, was kept in a public lavatory, before being paraded over 100 times through the streets of Beijing, while being verbally and physically attacked. On one occasion, he was rewarded for opposing the beating of his wife by a young Red Guard by being smashed over the head. While not actually killed in the CR, the stress and loss of face were hardly conducive to good health, and he died, under house arrest, in 1972.

Liu Shaoqi's is the real cause célèbre of rapidly disappearing power. This, after all, had been a man closely associated with Mao from the earliest days of the Party. Someone who had been born only a few miles from Mao's own birthplace in Hunan province. A man famed and loved for his so-called simple ways, modesty and hard work. But, his perceived 'liberalism' and implementation of Soviet-type reforms were to be his undoing when the big bust up with the Russians happened in the early 1960s. Indirectly named a 'capitalist roader' in the first attacks of the CR, it was clear even to outsiders that Liu was the main moving target. By 1967, he was explicitly 'nailed' as the chief traitor, and a tirade of invective fell upon his head. His being simply too senior to be physically attacked, as other lesser targets were did not prevent zealous Red Guard groups storming the central party compound, Zhongnanhai and hauling him out to be denounced. His wife, Wang Guangmei, was famously paraded before a crowd with a necklace made of ping- pong balls and a pair of panto-esque high heel shoes on, to mock her visit to Indonesia a few years earlier during which she had been perceived as making the PRC lose face by wearing a slit-dress *qipao* when she met President Sukarno. Wang Guangmei's interrogation by the Red Guards was to be a seminal text amongst the Red Guards during the CR – a sort of advertisement of how the mighty had fallen and that anyone was available for such onslaughts, true to Mao's own first and only 'Big Character Poster' (one of the peculiar literary products of this period) to 'bombard the headquarters'.

From 1967, Liu's previous record as the President of the PRC, and the number two man, was erased. His own children were made to denounce him and he was sent back to his home province. His death in 1969 was, reportedly, from untreated cancer. By this time, his hair had grown long and his nails uncut for several months. In a curious example of doublethink, he was rehabilitated after Mao's death, at the same time as the Chairman was still formally lauded as the father of the nation and a true Marxist-Leninist hero.

The competition for power at the top levels of Chinese politics was never a pretty game, largely because so much was at stake. Mao exercised a level of influence and control that was simply unthinkable to the Western politicians who met him. Richard Nixon, during his meeting with the Chairman in 1972, was, according to biographer Stephen Ambrose, simply overwhelmed by the aura of the man, who at that time was but a shadow of his previous self. Mao had impressed Nixon because of the sense that 'with a wave of his hand, he could wipe out ten thousand people'. Nixon had also been impressed by the sight of Premier Zhou Enlai redoing the front of the *People's Daily* and remarking sardonically that he wished he were able to do the same to the front of the *Washington Post*, a paper just then beginning to draw blood from him over Watergate.[2]

---

2   Stephen E Ambrose, *Nixon: Ruin and Recovery, 1973–90*. London, 1992.

Power and Violence in the PRC

But another feature is more elemental. Politics and violence in the PRC have always been close bedfellows. Pretenders to power, when they did not succeed, were to meet gruesome deaths, giving birth to the saying, particularly popular during the Maoist period, that 'he who dares to unseat the emperor must be brave enough to die by the death of a thousand cuts'. The price of failure was annihilation. The acceptable face of Chinese Communism for many years, the wily Premier Zhou Enlai, was famed in the 1930s and 1940s during the Communist's bandit years, for ordering the extermination of relatives and families of those accused of treachery. Zhou certainly understood the value of loyalty. Far from being the moderating, calming voice that he was presented as after the whirlwind of the CR was over, research has shown Zhou to have been both fully aware and in many ways complicit, in the round up of intellectuals their persecution and sometimes execution. He was, as sinologist, Michael Schoenhals has argued, the head of the Central Case Examination Group, the top level organ that selected and then pursued 'enemies of the state' in the CR period – hardly the occupation of an innocent man.[3]

Mao, like Lyndon B Johnson in the US, prided himself on one thing and that was an ability to locate, and develop power. And he understood, fully, the relationship between the exercise of physical force and political power. His most famous quote, still, is the blunt assertion that 'power grows from the barrel of a gun'. This was, of course, a gross distortion. Mao's Communists did plenty of 'hearts and minds' work in their years of struggle. They were great propagandists, and they disseminated codes of conduct that meant that they looked after their key constituency – the peasants – very well. No nationalist-style looting and pillaging for the Red Army. The Communist cultivation of the arts of soft power after 1949 manifested itself in the myth of the selfless cadre, in campaigns like the 'Lei Feng' one, where a humble army soldier was lauded as the quintessence of selflessness and Party spirit, and in the dissemination of a narrative of Chinese history which showed that liberation for the good, downtrodden classes had at last been delivered, and now the main imperative was to maintain unity.

But in terms of acting as a trump card, access to and the ability to call on the loyalty of and use of military power was pretty much the key thing. PLA,

---

3   Michael Schoenhals, 'The Central Case Examination Group, 1966–79', *The China Quarterly*, March 1996,pp. 87–111.

after all, had been the deliverers of the nation from servitude. They had been the main force achieving the creation of the PRC in 1949. They had restored the country's national pride. Their work did not end in 1949. In moments of national crisis, the PLA was a symbol of resolution and unity. When the CR looked like it was tipping towards Civil War in 1967 and 1968, the PLA was drawn back into effectively running civilian government. Their political reliability, at least to Mao, was unquestionable. While the PLA were on his side, Mao was always safe.

This continued even after his death. The Chairmanship of the Central Military Commission (CMC) is regarded, to this day, as the crown jewel in the firmament of Chinese power. Former President, Jiang Zemin was seen as only having half-retired when he stopped being President, as he continued as Chairman of the CMC. But his handing over of this a couple of years later to Hu Jintao marked the real transition to the 'fourth generation of leaders'. Not that the people are as starry eyed about the glories of the PLA as they used to be. Regarded as largely neutral and acting in the people's favour for the first 40 years of the PRC's history, the PLA undertook a massive strike when they became embroiled in the Tiananmen Square Incident/Massacre in 1989, turning their weapons and tanks on students for the first time in the PRC's history. It transpired afterwards that this had been a contentious decision, with some divisions utterly opposed to getting involved. Only two crack battalions based outside Beijing, in the end, had heeded the call. Their reward would be personal thanks from the ageing Deng Xiaoping in 1989, when he bemoaned the 'inevitability' of such turbulence, and expressed tribute to the one part of Chinese society that would never stray.

After divesting itself of commercial interests, and ridding itself of many hundreds of thousands of personnel, the PLA is not quite the unifying force it once was. But it remains the final expression of the Party's control, and their ability, if needed, to get serious if there is any unwanted opposition. The gun may be wrapped in a velvet cover, and hidden under the seat, but it is still close to the exercise of power in the PRC. And looks likely to remain so.

For those who interact with the contemporary PRC, the scent and sights of power can be found everywhere. There is a clear semiotic code here, some of it inherited from the genealogy of power partially outlined above, some of it adapted to the modern communications technology so important to convey power and influence throughout the rest of the world. There is a geography of power. Wander in Beijing and you can sniff it in the air, often in the most surprising places. Not the Forbidden Palace, where it has long since moved on from. That is just a museum now. But go a little further, up the wide boulevard to the gate of the Zhongnanhai compound. This is where the real players now work and live. The scent of power there is strong and clear. For those who get beyond the guards posted at the entrance, the inside is a haven of undisturbed calm, the well preserved ancient buildings standing much as they must have when Mao and his gang were in power.

This is not a place for raised voices. It is a place for control. Meetings here follow a prescribed course, with the outcomes settled before they even start. Visiting foreign dignitaries are ushered into beautifully clean rooms, where rows of armchairs face each other and seating position is rigorously codified. Well presented waitresses pour out tea and hand out warm towels to mop the nervously sweating brows of visitors. Then, from behind a screen, the leader who has been arranged comes forth, followed by his (or her, though at the moment female Chinese leaders are few and far between) translators and advisors, who sit silently around him. The body language fits completely with the environment – control, command and calm display of authority. Welcoming words, well informed, eloquent comments on the subject at hand (trade, politics, art, take your pick.) Even on sensitive topics (Taiwan, Tibet) fluster is rare. The script is well prepared. The lines are set out well. The sight of a red faced, angry Li Peng haranguing the visiting American Secretary of State, Warren Christopher in the mid 1990s was an aberration that did nothing to help Li's widely (but perhaps mistakenly) negative image outside China. Display of anger is the last thing that might happen, at least in this rarefied environment. Both sides need to turn in a performance. Visiting politicians mention sensitive things like human rights or Tibet only in general terms. The response is almost always so generic as to be meaningless. The key thing is that each of these encounters must deliver 'atmospherics'. The slightest sign of favour – a warmer handshake, a few minutes added to the end of the meeting, a couple more 'heartfelt' laughs – are carried away as important signs of progress towards the great undefined, future goal.

Such power has an aloofness about it. Visitors from Hong Kong, famously, used to expose their pretensions to be culturally more able to understand their northern brethren by grabbing extended hands for a handshake with both of their own. Such actions betrayed servility, running counter to part of the code of conduct for such encounters, which was that both sides needed to play the game and preserve at least the semblance of equality, preserving each other's faces. Chinese leaders are masters of a certain self-deprecation that only bolsters their power. The message is simple. We can make faint jokes about ourselves because we can afford to.

The hand movements of leaders of the third generation like Jiang Zemin used to fascinate me – the way in which, as he spoke, he airily drew circles in the air, or flattened his hand out and pointed away as he emphasized a point. Bob Hawke, the Prime Minister of Australia in the 1980s was famed for his dextrous use of body language, especially his trick, when in a tight spot, of extending his palms and exposing his wrists almost in a gesture of supplication. Chinese leaders like to dig the air when they emphasize a point, their speech rising slightly, as they reach a crescendo (usually on points like emphasizing the 'greatness' of the PRC, its unity and its future).

Such performances can look arrogant, but on the whole they are an accepted part of the whole theatre of Chinese politicians and indeed, of any holders of power, commercial, intellectual, or social, in the PRC. Visitors with a smattering of experience are right to feel slightly short changed if they don't see this part of the tourist landscape like the Great Wall and the Terracotta Warriors. Not that there aren't variations. More aggressive officials in smaller provinces are adept at putting visitors in their place by taking mobile calls in the middle of a meeting, or simply talking away to their aides while their interlocutor is presenting some intricate fact. The message is always the same – you are in the presence of power. The thing you are talking about, that you want to do, is going to be decided by me. I, by the way, have power. Can't you tell?

Playing the *Guangxi* Game

Guangxi, or connections, is part of the China brand. But it is a shadowy concept, and one that comes close to fulfilling that requirement of all good semiotics, that a powerful sign is often an empty, indeterminate one. *Guangxi* extends over the whole social nexus, into every area of life in the PRC – and foreigners, or outsiders of any kind, need to buy into it, just as much as they need to buy Chinese yuan to survive. Everyone has their theory about *guangxi* – and their own personal list of who they know, and how useful they are. This is where they get grafted on to the whole power highway, looking and hunting for those who may be beneficial to them, and then working out ways they can get closer, and ingratiate themselves with these 'key players'. The initial gamble is to take a punt on who in the organization or entity you are dealing with has clout. There you come across the bewildering mismatch between what a person's title is, their formal position and whether or not they are powerful at all. The next step is to devise ways of, not too obviously, working towards these people, and getting beside them. That can involve anything from the lunches that are held to convey respect and flatter guests and dinners (extortionately expensive seafood meals are popular here), to being more imaginative and establishing whether they have children, and if they do, how they might be assisted in being educated abroad.

It is part of the PRC's sophistication that the sort of openly given brown envelopes (though here called red) customary in other parts of the world are not so common. Corruption with Chinese characteristics involves a careful calculation of preserving face versus an outright appeal to someone's greed and selfishness. Benefits in kind are a useful start off and the acceptance of them means, at least to most, the establishment of a mutually beneficial relationship. Trips abroad, for instance, and expensive gifts. But somewhere along the line, if it is pure corruption we are talking about, there will be a discrete 10 per cent tucked away for 'services'. Nothing said, nothing noticed.

The truly powerful in China are above all this and establishing relations with them requires much more than crude material goods – they have, after all, pretty much all they want. In these realms, at least you have to be talking about something that both sides really need and get benefit from – intellectual property, for instance, or political gain. A photo or meeting with a top-level leader is immensely useful, and casts reflected glory on you. To this end, powerful people are swamped when they appear at receptions, by those wanting to pose by them almost like waxworks, and snatch some of their political capital.

The writer, the late Anthony Sampson, wrote in the last *Anatomy of Britain* in 2004 that the greatest change in the power hierarchy in the UK over the last 40 years since he had been writing his five-yearly reviews was the shift of influence away from traditional elites like landowners, aristocrats, what is loosely called the establishment to the wealthy. In twenty-first century Britain, power was coming more and more to be equated with money. The more money, the more power.[4]

In the PRC, that journey (*sans*, of course, the aristocrats) has been similar, but far more extreme. The establishment of the Party and the Party elite, holding almost all the trump cards of influence and social prestige, has now been heavily diluted. Part of this comes from its loss of credibility during the CR. Part of it is simply the drift of history. In contemporary PRC, the power elite have had their ranks swollen by entrepreneurs, and the new wealthy, a group of people who were sworn enemies of the socialist project from 1949, but who have now been accommodated under the great paradox of

---

4   Anthony Sampson, *Who Runs This Place?: The Anatomy of Britain in the 21st Century*, London, 2004.

'Chinese market socialism'. Such figures can exercise God-like powers over whatever fiefdom they control, whether it is their factories, businesses, or within their sectors. In a culture now obsessed with material wealth and getting rich, these are the new superheroes, people who have achieved what could be called the modern Chinese dream and are part of the pantheon of heroes along with the old Party leaders.

Part of the paradoxical means by which this new elite exercise their power is by nurturing opaqueness as much as the former high-level leaders did. When the first few Fortune 100 lists were produced of the PRC's new mega-wealthy, they were sardonically nicknamed death lists because of the way they drew the attention of the authorities to the irregular tax–paying or commercial habits of those on the list. A good number of them were brought in and banged up.

But the march of dialectic materialist history continues apace and in 2002, private entrepreneurs were allowed to become Party members, with the new constitution acknowledging the 'contribution' of the new private sector. There was expediency in operation here. Without a private sector, it was hard to see where all the millions being laid off from rationalizing SOE were going to end up. The government had left the decision to the last moment, but in the end it had no choice.

New Kids on the Block: The New Chinese Capitalists

The power of this new class of Chinese capitalists, while ostensibly purely commercial, of course has a profoundly political cast – and in bringing them into the tent, one might argue that the Party was operating on the principle that it was better to have them pissing from the inside out rather than the other way round. But the existence of this increasing band of the wealthy poses some interesting issues for the mapping out of power geography in the PRC now and what will happen in the future. These people are, after all, increasingly influential. Even more worrying, the state needs them, and needs them to increase. But at the moment, it couldn't possibly allow them to articulate anything that might sound like a political programme. No joining the dots between the practice of capitalism and democratization. And no desire for politicized entrepreneurs à la Richard Branson or Anita Roddick. The power of entrepreneurs, therefore, while symbolically immensely potent, is still neatly circumscribed. And one of the great games in the next few years is to see how these two, seemingly contradictory paths, are kept together.

For the rest, though, entrepreneurs show surprisingly similar character traits to political leaders. They bustle around in expensive, chauffeur driven cars (with, of course, the windows heavily tinted), hold similar kind of meetings with officials, where they sit in plush armchairs, surrounded by their assistants and lackeys, declaring humility while signalling the precise opposite to any visiting dignitary they deign to meet who is passing by. They play their cards close to their chest, and operate in a way that adds yet one more contradiction to the myriads that exist to make the PRC what it is today – advertising their wealth and prestige while also slightly denying and concealing it. So the Rolexes, Bentleys, and chairman's rooms dripping with gold plated furniture are all visible – but massive mansions, private helicopters, the sorts of trapping of mega wealth tolerable in the west, are all out of sight. In the PRC, it is OK to be wealthy in a certain way.

Those on a power hunt in the PRC can expect many twists and turns. Not only can power suddenly evaporate and vanish, swallowed up by the force of other greater, more compelling powers, but it can also be self-consuming. In the great game of self-serving corruption so popular in the PRC now, there is a right way and a wrong way – and you have to avoid stepping into the zone where suddenly all those things you were doing which were OK a moment before suddenly become mortal sins, and you are devoured by the dreaded legal system, a system that, in its perversity and capriciousness, makes Charles Dickens's 'Chancery World' in his later novels look benign. For the vast majority, though, the experience of power is to be passive sufferers of it, rather than acquirers of it in any meaningful sense. The world is full of those agents of the state who, while they may not be half as important as they used to be, can still do much to make your life hell. There are the Public Security Officials, armed with vaguely worded regulations, who can swoop upon your business or your private life and claim some terrible element of immorality and illegality, dressed up as anti-Party behaviour. Counter-revolutionaries may be a thing of the past, on the whole, but 'hoodlums' or social troublemakers are now the catch-all terms by which to speak about those who are being nabbed. There are the officials, who you need to arrange some kind of administrative business through, who can lead you on a merry dance around a million and one impediments and irregularities if you get on the wrong side of them, denying you that one final piece of paper to get you to where you want to go. And there is that dark undergrowth of observers and watchers, the 30 thousand people in Beijing alone monitoring what people may be watching on the internet, ready to dive into sight from their hiding places when you violate one of the daily changing rules you may not even have been aware of. I heard only this year that 600 of Beijing's taxi drivers are in fact in the employ of the dreaded `Security Department', finishing off their night shift by dutifully filling out reports on the day's `casual' conversations and the conclusions about `public mood' that can be drawn from these. Stalin himself would have been proud of such attention to detail.

And once one of these agents pushes you into what one can poetically call the Chinese pit, the place of the disowned and disenfranchised, then you will experience a wholly different kind of power. The power, for instance, of those who can exploit you with impunity in the new PRC; the power of those who can incarcerate you, and, while incarcerated, literally do you to death with precious little comeback. And the power of those who can take away everything you have, with no explanation and only the most painfully slow and uncertain routes to reparation. For these, power is encapsulated in the grim Amnesty International reports, where consistent records are kept of the menus of humiliation and torture extended to those welcomed into the club of those who do not matter and whose lives are worth nothing.

The one consolation you may have should you ever descend to such places, deep beneath the surface of the new Chinese universe, with its gleaming city-skyscraper smiles and high ways to prosperity and development, is that the power game in contemporary PRC is, in many ways, arbitrary, and that all of the rules of its conduct and manifestation outlined above are contingent and could change tomorrow. And like with any game, those who are masters of it and are winning today, can quite quickly become the losers, and fall to the bottom of the pit tomorrow. Politicians, entrepreneurs, business people and local leaders – however high they may go, there is always the slight threat, the chance that with one foot misplaced, they could fall. The best tactic is to blindly carry on, in the hope that, while such fears can never be finally dispelled, at least they can be ignored or forgotten and the nightmare will never happen.

These power structures and characteristics seem so embedded that it is almost impossible to imagine the PRC being the PRC without them, rather like trying to imagine a greenhouse without glass. Whether 'internationalisation', globalization, and continuing opening up will do much to change these is a moot question. One thing is certain. For such a power structure to change there will be painful convulsions and redirections of energy. The attempt by Chinese companies, for instance, to export their power structures and relationship behaviour abroad will not carry very far. It is unlikely in the next decade that we will see manuals about Chinese management practice the way we did 15 years ago about Japan. Once bitten, twice shy. But instead of airily assuming that the Chinese need to do all the running, if they want to internationalize, perhaps there will be more attempts by outsiders to understand their own internal dynamics. The role of outsiders, and how they can and cannot influence the great Chinese system, is looked at in the next chapter.

CHAPTER EIGHT:
THE KINDNESS OF STRANGERS:
'OUTSIDERS' AND BEING CHINESE

Intimately involved with the question of being Chinese and what that means, is the issue of being not Chinese – foreign. In 'our' encounter with Chinese as outsiders, we will need to wrestle more and more with who Chinese are, what they mean to us, and what, in the end, we think we mean to them.

Foreigners and Chinese are one of the great polarities of the contemporary world. To some, Chinese are a threat. To others, they are people that aren't easy to understand. But the days when in fact it didn't really matter who the Chinese were, as they were locked away inside their fortress like country, are long over. Like it or not, even if we don't join the millions of tourists now flocking to the PRC, they are now coming in increasing numbers over here – as students, business people, tourists and skilled migrants. The dialogue of 'outsiders' and 'insiders' that has carried on down the centuries has entered a new phase.

And as I will argue in this chapter, the impact of foreigners and Chinese on each other has not been negligible. The guiding ideology of the PRC for the last half-century has been a foreign import – Marxism-Leninism. The red blooded capitalist now thriving on the PRC's streets is the latest manifestation of the industrial revolution and the technical and social changes it inaugurated two centuries ago in the West. Technologies that originated in dynastic China – inventions and discoveries ranging from fireworks to paper – have run full circle, so that the western innovations in Information and Technology (IT) and bioscience, and, of course, nuclear technology, are now reaching back to the PRC, profoundly changing its nature. Producing engineers, mathematicians and technologists by the hundreds of thousands each year, it seems only a matter of time before the West will be hunting in the PRC for cutting edge new ideas, rather than the other way round.

How can 'outsiders' react to this gradual change around? With welcoming arms or trepidation? Once more, we have to understand some recent history to really be able to make sense of the idea of how foreigners are viewed and how they are likely to fare, in the new PRC of the twenty-first century.

Friends and Enemies

It might help to start off by looking at the term 'friend' and what it means in the PRC? The Chinese for friend, '*pengyou*', whenever I heard it, always seemed laden with problems and questions. Not that 'friend' is that precise in English, but in the PRC, where so many are talking about the value and importance of relations, and where the value of people to each other is always being calculated in the great stock exchange of human worth, it raised to me the question of what sort of friend a friend in the PRC was. A useful friend? A true friend? A close friend? Or a friend who wasn't a friend at all? Is it basically what you called everyone? In the PRC, following that logic, everyone is friends with each other. And that in an environment where trust (for reasons I'll elaborate later) was in short supply.

In the keywords of the Chinese social lexicon, 'friend' ranks up there in complexity and hybridity with 'power', 'unity' and 'nationality'. When I first lived in the PRC in the 1990s, I was warned by someone who declared himself to be 'my friend', to trust no one, only listen, never say what I thought about anything and to always try and work out why someone was trying to make friends with me. A decade later, another 'friend' insisted that I should never let people know that I spoke or understood Chinese, that in meetings I should only ask questions and not speak about what I thought, and that I should 'mystify' those I dealt with. Trying to practice this lasted an afternoon, as in effect, it consigned me to perpetual silence, and meant I was hostage to the undiluted thought streams of those I was encountering.

The idea of 'friend' as applied to foreigners becomes particularly complicated. All foreigners, as placards in the new Beijing declare, are 'friends'- though it doesn't take much to work out that this can only apply to some foreigners. Japanese, for instance, are pretty clearly foreigners – but in the last year or so, because of the continuing residue from the Japanese-Chinese history during the 1930s and 1940s, Chinese, in many cases, have not considered themselves particularly friendly towards Japanese. This has manifested itself in riots, vehement attacks on Internet sites and some clearly government led anti-Japanese campaigns. When the Chinese Embassy was ('accidentally') bombed in Belgrade in 1999, foreigners were certainly not feeling regarded as friends, especially if they were American or British (the British embassy still bore the marks of stones hurled at it during the demonstrations from that time in 2005). The experience of some non-white races in the PRC has also been less than comfortable.

In the great modern discourse of friendship, friends should be 'frank' with each other, able to talk about difficult issues, so that their relationship can endure these and be enriched and enlarged by it. But the eagerness with which the Chinese publicly declare some kinds of outsiders friends is still seductive, and means that those exposed to this 'warmth and hospitality' initially can get disorientated by it. The more cynical think that might be the whole point of it – an attempt to put foreigners off their guard, motivated by the desire to win them over and recruit them as it were. We are back to my 'friend' in 1995 telling me to always be working out why people were trying to make friends with me. Like it or not, this complicated interplay between insiders and outsiders, Chinese and foreigners seems set to play well into the future.

What does 'Foreigner' Mean?

Being a foreigner poses very interesting issues and questions in the PRC, as it does anywhere. Being foreign, the status of being an outsider is always a very specific and special place. In Japan, where even third generation Koreans are considered 'aliens' (they still need to bear the charmingly named Alien Registration Cards) there is a firmly stated homogeneity, almost unashamed. When I taught in rural Japan at a high school in the early 1990s (Japan remains, through the scheme I was on, the Japan English Teacher (JET) programme, the largest single employer of recently graduated British nationals) I remember a fellow teacher solemnly telling me that, of course, as a white foreigner, I was respected and looked up to – but fellow Asians were considered beneath most Japanese and Africans, well they were barely worth thinking about. As an island nation, effectively closed off for several centuries until the Meiji Reforms in the 1860s, Japan had at least some historical foundation on which to base its fervent declarations of homogeneity. But for the many China's that have existed, with their shifting borders, their '55 national minorities', their shared borders with over a dozen other countries, this concept of who is 'within' and who counts as an outsider is much more amorphous.

If we restrict talk of foreign experience specifically to European, or at least Western European perspectives, then we can see a gradual process of mutual mythologizing. There are the canonical texts of the very early Western experiences of the Far East and the Chinese empires. Marco Polo, for instance, in the thirteenth century, records in his '*Travels* his visit to the fabulous city of Xanadu, summer capital of the great Khan, grandson of Genghis. But as Francis Wood has persuasively argued, Marco Polo may never even have been to China and the whole account might have been as fantastical as the description of the fabulous Xanadu found in Purchas's *Pilgrimage* a few centuries later which served as the basis for Samuel Coleridge's opium-inspired 'Kubla Khan' fragment.[1]

Edward Said famously talked of this process of mythologizing the Orient, both through straight storytelling and also simply through creating a whole discourse or corpus of 'learning' that supports the idea of a specific kind of other. His focus was on the Orient as in what is now more commonly called the Middle East – though much the same could be said of the further Orient, in what is now labelled East Asia.[2] The pivotal moment for this experience of mutual incomprehension and its mythologizing on both sides was the Lord Macartney delegation to the Court of the Qianlong emperor in 1793, of which he wrote a full account, and which contained the famous encounter where the emperor (after a great deal of dextrous negotiation on both sides to preserve face – Macartney refused to kowtow to the emperor and this had to be circumvented by various other tactics that spare people's humiliation or mean they lose credibility) simply declared that the Qing China that existed then had no need of the goods and trade from the empire of George III.

One of the impacts of this meeting was that, for much of the following century or so, Qing China was regarded as insular, arrogant, self-contained and the Chinese as having a closed, excluding relationship with outsiders. Lydia Liu, Professor of Chinese Studies at the University of Michigan, has written in detail about this mutual invention in her *The Clash of Empires*. It was commonplace in much nineteenth century literature about Qing China that the Chinese regarded outsiders as barbarians, people culturally far beneath the Chinese. But, as Liu shows in her analysis of the term, '*Yi*' which signified 'barbarian' in English translations of Chinese texts, in fact the character had no such meaning. It was better translated as 'foreigner', or 'outsider'. Transforming this one term into the much more emotive, judgemental 'barbarian' in the English versions created the mindset it was aimed at by distortion of the original. This process was taken to a further level simply when rules were laid down by foreign presences in Qing China

---

1   Frances Wood, *Did Marco Polo Go to China?*, London 1996.
2   Edward W. Said, *Orientalism*, New York 1979.

stipulating that the term '*yi*' *had* to be translated as 'barbarian', excluding any other notion. The dynamics here, therefore, was that foreigners were almost dictating a negative image of themselves in the other language to bolster their own claim that they were viewed negatively.[3]

With this sort of history, it is no surprise that communications between those who regard themselves as 'Chinese' and Western Europeans, at least in this case, has a rich archive of mutual misunderstanding. In twentieth century discourse produced by the Communists, especially after 1949, Europeans, and Americans, were placed in the paradoxical position of being both reviled and envied, despised and admired. The narrative of 'exploitation' and suffering of China under the imperialist powers, as they were labelled, leading up to the Opium Wars in the 1840s and the unequal treaties was a constant source of animosity, compounded by the Boxer Rebellion of 1900 that saw steep reparations demanded from the Chinese (the residue of which still fund scholarships for British and Chinese students through the Universities China Committee in London to this day), the sacking of the Summer Palace in Beijing, and then the settlement at the end of World War I that again carved Republican China into spheres of influence.

1949 was the moment of the new history, one important plank of which was simply that from now on 'foreigners would be used for Chinese ends'. There was recognition that at least in terms of technology, Westerners had pulled ahead. They needed to be emulated, and beaten. Those that airily declare that the PRC's great attempt to catch up with the Western developed and industrialized societies started in 1978 forget that this was always a guiding ambition of the Communists and indeed was the inspiration behind the doomed Great Leap Forward, which was aimed at letting the PRC overtake the UK and US in steel production in three years.

The post-1949 collective effort to catch up with the West, at least in terms of technology and scientific knowledge, went hand in hand with an increasing closure of the PRC to the outside world. The reasons for this remain controversial. Some argue that the West 'lost the PRC' and missed a chance to build open and good relations with the new country, which was, from the outset, keen to have dialogue. They cite the famous encounter between Dean Rusk, US Secretary of State under President Eisenhower and Chinese Premier Zhou Enlai, at the Geneva Conference in 1954. Dean Rusk simply refused to shake the extended hand of the Chinese Premier. But others feel that the Chinese were set on closing the doors quite early on,

3 *The Clash of Empires: The Invention of China in Modern World Making*, Harvard 2005.

that their outlook was necessarily nationalist and introspective, and that the decades of limited involvement with foreigners was a continuation of what had happened in the previous centuries when foreigners had been restricted to specific zones and allowed only limited access to locals.

What is undeniable is that, by the period of the CR, the doors of the PRC were tightly closed. There were a handful of 'foreign guests' (more on these later), but the large contingent of Russian specialists had been booted out after the row with the USSR in the late 1950s. Only Albania, it seemed, maintained friendly relations. Any visitors needed to lobby exhaustively for their right to visit, had their visits tightly controlled, and were only able to report back on the tiny segment of the PRC that they were allowed to see. Most of the time, they needed to read between the lines, or fill in fairly massive gaps. Hong Kong was one of the few vantage points, with the testimony of refugees and visitors who had somehow made it there. It was from here that that honourable fraternity of outsiders, the PRC watchers, made their forays. Ex-British Ambassador to China, Sir Christopher Hum, when he first visited the PRC in 1970, crossed the border from Hong Kong into the Mainland (there were no direct air routes then) with only two other people. Visitors returning issued lengthy reports of their stays, which were delivered to a world starved of information about the Real PRC, invariably described as 'behind the Bamboo curtain'.

The True Foreign Friends: A History

There were another group of foreigners, who occupied a much more privileged position. Those who, for some reason, had stayed on since 1949. People like Americans Sidney Rittenberg or Sidney Shapiro, or New Zealander Rewi Alley. Their motives, in each case, varied. Many were deeply sympathetic to the great socialist experiment. Some, like journalist Agnes Smedley, had been observers of the epic struggle to attain power from the earliest days. Alley was a fascinating case – from farming stock, he was gay and life in the PRC at least offered him some freedom from judgement. He was to be a tireless promoter of the regime till his death well into his nineties in 1989, producing lengthy books on the situation 'as it really was' from within the PRC. Whether these people had much more perspective than those who enjoyed brief visits is another matter. Anne Maire Brady has written a good account of the phenomenon of foreign friends based in the

PRC.[4] At least until the CR they lived carefully protected lives, partly because of their use as propaganda or publicity tools. Some of them, like Rittenberg, were to fall foul of the changed political winds in the CR, becoming too fervent for their own good. In his account afterwards of the long years when others had left, Rittenberg wrote about the lengthy spells he spent in prison as a result of seizing Radio Beijing in 1967.[5] David Crook, a British anthropologist who had, with his wife, written accounts of life in reforming rural China in the 1940s and 1950s, was also to be incarcerated, emerging in the mid 1970s as a lexicographer (English language consultant of what remains one of the best Chinese-English dictionaries, despite containing some choice CR slogans as examples of phrase and word usage).

This group were the acceptable face of foreigners – proof, to those inside the PRC, that Maoism had indeed an international reach, and that the power of its ideology was sweeping over other countries and peoples. Some of them still live in the PRC to this day, with remarkable memories of all they have seen in the last 55 years. They were the vanguard of the great swarms of foreigners who now live, work and play in every conceivable part of the PRC.

The PRC has been thoroughly colonized now. The floodgates opened in the 1980s. In those days, the first Lonely Planet guide sounded like a description of another universe. It contained fierce deprecations of the Chinese habit of 'spitting from open windows on buses', playing their TVs loudly, gawping at foreigners, surrounding them in great crowds, and shrieking out 'hello' from hundreds of yards in the distance. Anyone reading these fearsome warnings deserved a medal to set foot in the land where there was a separate money system for foreigners (the dreaded Foreign Exchange Certificates, phased out in 1994), where arranging phone calls sometimes took a whole day, and where getting train tickets was like entering a lottery, with only a few lucky winners.

And these were just the practical problems. Then there was the great mental wall, the barriers of trust and suspicion. Foreigners, after all, in the discourse of the CR in particular, were simply the Enemy. It was they who had imported into the PRC pernicious thoughts, and were hell-bent on the collapse of the whole system, ready for the triumphant return of KMT (Kuomintang Nationalist Party) leader, Chiang Kaishek, across the Straits in the island of Formosa/Taiwan. The Russians even had the temerity, in

---

4   *Making the Foreign Serve China: Managing Foreigners in the People's Republic* New York, 2003.
5   *The Man Who Stayed Behind*, New York 2003.

1969, to mount a small attack across the northern border of Heilongjiang Province, a skirmish that was presented in CR pamphlets as sure proof that the rest of the world were out to get at the PRC, and no quarter should be given.[6] Such a history had left massive barriers in understanding in the 1980s. Fox Butterfield, a Canadian journalist based in Beijing in the early 80s, wrote a typical account of the sort of walls and impediments to having anything like a normal relationship with the Chinese at this time.[7] Foreigners were kept to compounds, guarded, observed, watched, their rubbish sifted through and their phone calls monitored. Unregulated contact was dangerous, with the good chance of those you reached out to being banged up as counter-revolutionaries, accused of being spies because of their contact with you.

Those foreigners who stayed in China long-term were interesting. Not the official PRC friends, but what could be called the second generation, who had come there in the first phase of the Opening Up Period in the 1980s. For them, as there were more, there had been none of the cosseting and privileges of the group present since 1949. They had fought harder battles to convince those they lived amongst that their motives were innocent. This was slightly ingenuous because a large number that came to work as teachers were, in fact, Christian missionaries going under another name, and proselytizing in the only way they could. An American, of partially American Indian origins, who I came across in Inner Mongolia in 1995 was a good example. A man who had come a decade before, and moved from city to city, working as a teacher, a businessman and now a student again. From a distance he looked quite Chinese, in his PLA-surplus coat, and Lei-Feng style hat. He talked in a low voice, with a slightly haunted look about him, like he was in perpetual flight from microphones. 'The Chinese,' he said once, 'are my closest friends, and my worst enemies'. With such polarized thoughts, he had settled into an oddly antagonistic relationship with his long-term hosts, frequently (and in the small town we were based famously) having 'run ins' with various kinds of authorities, who showed patience with him far in excess of what a similarly truculent Chinese in the West would have enjoyed. But his reckoning, when it came, was short and sharp. He was thrown out of the country, I heard, a couple of years later, ostensibly for 'visa violations', though of course the gossip in the town put it down to the definite intelligence that he had (of course) been a spy all along.

---

6   It seems likelier now that this 'attack' was instigated more on the Chinese side than the Russian.

7   *China: Alive in the Bitter Sea*, London 1983.

A foreigner in the PRC, therefore, to this day needs to grapple a bit with the residue of this lack of trust. Things are easier now, but there is still a real ambiguity about being a foreign friend, which goes to the heart of the nature of intimacy and the meaning of relationships in the New China. Foreigners, it must be remembered, live in two worlds. Even the long-term ones are only partially accepted. There is this fervently proclaimed myth of being 'real Chinese' and foreigners, in the end, can never quite get there. They can be accorded the privilege (according to what they are doing, who they are speaking to, and what they are saying) of 'understanding China', even being a 'true friend of China'. But the idea that a European foreigner, for instance, might 'naturalise' and become Chinese in the way that a Chinese immigrating to the UK can do so after several years fulfilling various criteria – that still seems way off. Like the Japanese, the Taiwanese and the Koreans, the Chinese set fearsome barriers for acquiring one of their passports – a paradox picked up on in the context of visas by a LSE academic who found that the more repressive the regime, on the whole, the less people wanted to visit and the less easy it was to get visas or travel documents to go to the place (witness the DPRK (Democratic People's Republic of Korea)).[8]

What Impact do We Have?

The days of enclosure, when the Chinese seemed to be locked on the other side of a wall, and contact with them was minimal and highly managed, are now long over. There is enough exposure and contact for both sides to not only know about each other more, but also to irritate and, at the same time, demystify. It's hard to maintain those tired old myths of the inscrutable, homogenous Chinese when they are filling our university class rooms, buying companies and factories here and producing over 50 per cent of our consumer goods, and giving daily evidence of their being, in many ways, very similar to us.

History should give us some clues. But the pattern of paradox that has been described elsewhere in this book recurs here. In the past, dynasties as far back as the Tang over a millennium ago have swung from real openness to outsiders to introversion and closure. Emperor Qianlong's reply to

---

8   Eric Neumayer, *Unequal Access to Foreign Space* available at http://www.lse.ac.uk/collections/geographyAndEnvironment/whosWho/profiles/neumayer/pdf/Visarest rictionsarticle.pdf, accessed 16 May 2006.

Macartney in 1793, while often trotted out, was perhaps a report of simple commercial sense. At that time, the Chinese simply didn't feel the want or need for imported goods. That was only to change through the enforced disaster of the opium trade half a century later. Contemporary addictions to imported cigarettes (the PRC is one of the few markets in the world where the rate of smokers in accelerating) have a haunting parallel to this earlier trade pattern.

The dialogues between the Chinas that have existed and the Wests that have interacted with it have, therefore, been complicated. Both sides have gained, and both sides have experienced nasty shocks. That pattern of ups and downs has only intensified in the last two decades. The 1980s were high points, when outsiders genuinely felt the PRC was on the path to democracy and reform. 1989 was the nasty shock that reminded people that the script they had prepared was not the one that the PRC was going to run its act to. This left a bad taste throughout the 1990s. In the 2000s, both sides have woken up to the realization that, with globalization, we can do as much harm as good to each other. The time for slammed closed doors is long past.

Credible observers split into two camps. One believes that outsiders have, in the last century, had next to no real impact on the Chinese. What they have wanted, they have taken and then adapted for use in China. Even the ideology of Marxism-Leninism has been reformulated as something with 'Chinese characteristics'. The PRC is different, they say and nothing from outside can last long without being modified. Others feel that in fact the country is a massive opportunity – a complicated empty space highly receptive to external influence. They point to the massive industrialization of the last two decades that is making the country more and more like its models abroad.

In fact, it is indisputable that some external imports more than hit the spot. Playing their cards right, foreigners can have influence far beyond what perhaps they merit. Foreign brands are placed above Chinese ones. Foreign companies are respected for their business operations above Chinese ones. The refrain that the PRC is corrupt and over complicated comes from more than one mouth in the PRC today. Foreigners seem to simplify things. Relationships with them, either in business or in other areas, seem less fraught than relationships with fellow locals.

Strategic engagement over the next decade, therefore, might well have a far greater impact than expected. In fact we might get a China that has all the extremes of our own societies and none of the positives – fearsomely materialistic, unstable through comprehensive privatization, with the same issues of drug use, crime and alienation that have plagued Western societies.

A PRC on the template of Shenzhen would be a fearsome sight. And in fact, by then, more and more of us, our companies, our products, our institutions, will be reliant on Chinese support. We might well be in a position then to ask whether the problem wasn't how outsiders can influence the PRC, but how the West can combat the influence of the Chinese.

CHAPTER NINE:
THE CHINESE ECONOMY

The glue holding the variant Chinas apart in the twenty-first century is the worship and commitment, to the unifying narrative of the economy. You can sit, as a Chinese or a visitor, in the various Starbucks colonizing Beijing, holding your jewel encrusted mobile phone in your hand, irritated about the tardiness of your chauffeur outside, remembering the thousand dollar meal of sea food that left you hungry from the night before, loudly declaring that the Communist Party sucks, and that it is time for a bit of democracy. It is unlikely that the myriad secret police and other surveillers of the imminent insurrection in the new Chinese State would bother much. After all, they have worked out that people like you have too much to loose if it all goes down. But too much politics is a bad thing in the PRC, and there are key words, little phrases, areas of sensitivity, emanating from The Zone, that mysterious guarded territory of the unmentionable and unnameable that from time to time sucks in those who have been a little too adventurous in their activity and thought.

In the CR, politics was put in command. The discourses of politics, of class struggle, social advancement, progress and state command dominated everything. People let politics seep deep into their hearts. But there, of course, it nearly broke them. Most people in the new PRC are refugees from politics. They articulate indifference. They have become married to the great discourse of the economy. That is pretty safe. If you go on too much about politics, you will likely as not fall foul. It really is the economy, stupid, and banging on about anything else is likely to end in tears.

And how people talk about the Chinese economy – all the time, all over the place, all strenuously declaring a series of truths and givens about it. In the dynasties before, they built the Great Wall, or the Forbidden Palace or the Terracotta Warrior tombs. These days, they are building the Chinese Economy. And unlike the Great Wall, the effects of the Chinese economy really are visible from the moon.

The Basics

These are the givens. In the last two decades, since the narrative of the Opening Up and Reform Process under Deng Xiaoping, the PRC has moved to the world's fourth largest economy, lifting over 300 million people from relative or absolute poverty, posting average growth rates of 10 per cent per year, becoming the second largest attractor of Foreign Direct Investment and holding the largest foreign exchange reserves in the world. The Chinese are in line, according to Goldman Sachs, to be the world's largest economy in the 2030s, if not before. Factories in the South of China produce, from single plants, something like 90 per cent of the world's microwave ovens, half of its socks, most of its software and electronic goods. Former Premier, Zhu Rongji simply announced in the 1990s that the PRC was the factory of the world. Those wandering around the frenetic business parks and factory bases in Guangzhou or Zhejiang would be inclined to agree. 90 per cent of the great consumer monster Wal-Mart's goods are made in China.

All of this is declared with great fervour by party officials whenever they get the chance – at openings of joint ventures, at visits by delegations abroad, during high-level political visits and when visitors come through. History is respected by the initial solemn announcement that 'the Opening Up of reforms under Deng Xiaoping has produced great results'. Then you had better clear out of the way before a barrage of statistics and 'facts' rain down upon your head. Steel production up by x percent, average consumer spending index up by y per cent, amount of contractual direct investment increased by z billion renminbi… Bureaucrats in Beijing offices map out these myriad statistics, mopping them up from whatever source they can find them, scattering them around like confetti at a wedding.

The Story of A Statistic

Those that try to track these dizzying statistics back to something manageable, have a hard time. Even simple statistics seem to tell multiple stories. Take a very simple one. British Investment in the PRC, a statistic I mentioned above. Here is a very easy tale. The UK is the largest EU investor. There is 20 billion pounds worth of investment. There are over 3,000 UK/China joint ventures. This figure looks good, and is a great advertisement for the UK PLC.

More sceptical voices, though, would wonder about this claim. It seemed there were a lot more visible German, or French companies in China than British ones. Carrefour seemed to be opening everywhere. German engineers looked like they were setting up new joint ventures every week. Whenever we needed to trot out examples of British investment, it was a little more difficult – BP (British Petroleum), Shell, Rolls Royce, Vodafone, some banks and Airbus (the UK side – for us, it was always primarily a British company, with residual European interest!). And our airy comment would be that, for sure, of that 20 billion pounds of investment, half was yet to be fulfilled though it had been contractually committed. And of the ten billion left, almost 90 per cent was in the good and capable hands of BP, Shell and Vodafone.

To assuage these nagging doubts about what exactly British companies were doing in China, we did come up with the, at the time, logical idea of going to the European department of what was then the MOFTEC (amalgamated, with some other ministries, into the Ministry of Trade in 2003). MOFTEC themselves had no such grand list of British companies. In fact, their official said, they assumed we would have that. Don't British companies need to report to the government in the UK before they invest abroad? We patiently explained that the UK had long since ceased to be a state led economy and that, in fact, companies were likely not to want to tell the government what they were doing unless they really had to. It was entirely their business.

For this illusive list of British companies active in China, we had two options. Ask a researcher in Beijing, who had produced reports on the nature of US and Japanese investment in China, to do a similar job for us. But his asking fee was over 50 thousand pounds. Or simply go to each of the Department of Foreign Trade and Economic Co-operation offices in China's 31 provinces and autonomous regions, and ask them what lists they had of UK/Chinese joint ventures in their areas.

A stab at the second option turfed up some interesting points. On trips to Gansu, Inner Mongolia and Qinghai, I did ask specifically for these lists. And when I arrived, I was handed neat printouts with the companies active in the area. But this exercise ended up raising more questions than answers. The lists of British investments included names like the Taiwan Cake Corporation, or British Virgin Islands Technology Limited. It became pretty clear then that what was collated, at least in these provinces, were simply any investments, direct or indirect, that could be vaguely connected via offshore accounts to the UK. There the connection ended. Xinjiang were more forthcoming in their rendition of what British investment they had. The sole investment, they said, was a coffee shop in the remote town of Kashgar partly owned, or run, or set up, by a Brit. That was it.

This is a simple account of a simple statistic. But it shows that every statistic, in its superficial simplicity, tells a story. The most epic statistic of China's great expansion story over the last two decades has been, of course, the growth rate. In the 1980s, China frequently posted rates in double digits. Shenzhen, one of the first Special Economic Zones, racked up figures in the thirties and forties during its early years. But as Nicholas Lardy commented in his sceptical 1998 book, *China's Unfinished Economic Revolution*, all of these fantastic figures were starting from a low base. And, more intriguingly, even in the grim years of the 1960s and 1970s, China's official growth rate figures were, amazingly, OK.[1]

It wouldn't be the first time that, amongst all the voices of euphoria and glee, someone mused about what the actual basis for these figures are. In the last five years, credible voices ranging from the British *Economist* magazine to Joe Studwell, author of *The China Dream* have questioned where these numbers came from and dared to wonder whether they might not be half what they actually are. Gordon Chang, Shanghai-based author of *The Coming Collapse of China*, even went one step further in his dystopian analysis and questioned the whole great edifice of China's economic performance.[2]

The visible signs of China's development are not hard to find. Beijing and Shanghai are awash with huge new buildings, flashy cars, restaurants heaving with people and plush shopping malls selling branded goods. There is definitely a wealthy middle- class, who have been the real winners in the Reform Process. But as someone curtly joked a few years back, you know you have been in the PRC a decent length of time and are relatively acclimatized, when someone tells you poker faced that they only earn the equivalent of 300 dollars a month, but are able to drive around in a new Mercedes (remembering, of course, that imported cars are far more expensive in the PRC due to the current import tariffs, though under WTO these are meant to be relaxed). Chinese are more willing to brag about the enormous amounts of money they have, but the exact extent of this wealthy class is very contentious. The late Gerald Segal, in his 1999 essay 'Does China Matter' sourly noted that we might be talking about a consumer base no bigger than the adult population of Belgium. Are these people really enough for foreign companies to shed their billions of pounds of consumer goods and merchandise to?[3]

---

1   Nicholas Lardy, *China's Unfinished Economic Revolution*, Washington 1998.
2   Gordon Chang, *The Coming Collapse of China*, New York 2001.
3   Gerald Segal, 'Does China Matter', in *Foreign Affairs*, September–October 1999.

China's Second, Third and Fourth Coming

Joe Studwell, in *The China Dream* looks at the history of this excitement about the imminent Chinese 'advent'.[4] It has been anticipated for a long time. Even in the 1930s, the textile manufacturers of Manchester were inspired by the thought that if one Chinaman wanted to extend his jacket by only an inch, it would increase the output of cotton from their mills by millions. That massive potential (and here the emphasis is on the word 'potential') of the Chinese market has been a haunting spectre for generations, suppressed by the closure of the PRC under Mao, but now back at full strength. It is, in fact, one of the abiding myths that make up this thing we now call the PRC, along with the idea of it 'standing up' mentioned above. There is a fascination about this story, one that captures the imaginations of people outside. Like most stories, there is resistance to giving it up for a more sober alternative.

And the Chinese economy is the domain of this great hunt. It is here that the seekers, and finders, losers and keepers, dreamers and realists, collide. A great behemoth over which statisticians, economists, business moguls and politicians crawl, producing from time to time with mighty cries of 'eureka' some sign that they have found or located something tangible, real, true, about the enormous creature they are trying to grapple with, and tame – the PRC's potential.

Those judged 'successful' in dealing with this great beast, are regarded, and indeed act, like they have returned from a conversation with the Gorgon's Head, and not been turned to stone. Like finders of pots of gold at the end of the rainbow, the business community in Beijing or Shanghai whisper about the stories of those who have 'succeeded' and made 'loads of money'. But more often than not, as Studwell himself pointed out, to the simple question, Do you make money in the PRC?, most business people from outside become remarkably coy and start telling evasive, slightly shamefaced stories about what is in the pipeline, and what contracts they have signed. In the great chase for the golden Chinese yuan, the signifiers of success are those 'with Chinese characteristics'. No money in the bank yet, but a 'promising' meeting with the Party Secretary of so-and-so, good signs from the lead official in a city in the back of beyond, excellent delegations to the UK, and a relationship with the grand daughter of an important general in the PLA. And all of this is leading somewhere, to the moment when the great giant stands up and the world shakes and the long awaited money sweeps over the heads of those who have waited so patiently.

---

4   Joe Studwell, *The China Dream*, London 2002.

Charles Dickens's Gradgrind in *Hard Times* asked for 'Facts, facts, facts' –
but statistics don't seem to fully assuage the doubters and really point to 'the
truth'. Walking around the booming cities, confronted with the physical
appearance of China's new wealth still leaves a lot of questions about where
all this money has come from, how much there is and how deep it goes. At
any one time, those gleaming, wonderful offices in Shenzhen are only 50 per
cent full. And what might look on the outside like glitzy top-notch splendour
reveals itself as jerry-built tack. This disjuncture between appearance and
reality seeps from the look of physical things to the real content of
Memorandums of Understanding and Contracts gaily signed and then down
to the actual business transacted. What is the reality of the Chinese
economy? Where are the facts, and how can they best be found?

The Never-Ending Story of the State

The seekers of truth must remember a couple of things before they start
their journey. They must remember this is an environment saturated by the
celebration of contradiction and paradox (see Chapter 3). So while the
Reform Process has, indeed, opened up the Chinese economy to direct
investment, and allowed the entrepreneurial spirit of the average Chinese to
take wing, this was built on a very specific foundation. From 1949, the
Chinese economy was a system run, directed, owned and promoted, by the
State. The State was everywhere, from the tiniest restaurant to the greatest
enterprises pumping out millions of tonnes of steel or iron. The state may
have retreated in the last two decades, but it has not gone away, and most
journeys into any Chinese entity have a surprising habit of ending up at the
doors of what look remarkably like State Owned Enterprises (SOE) no
matter what labels are hung upon then.

The hardy business people of that first age of the Chinese economy
needed to carry out deals with officials. There were not, despite having
entrepreneurs like the late Rong Yiren as members, business people to talk
to as such. These had been swept away, or had their labels changed, in the
great class clearout that ran from 1949. Capitalists, along with landlords and
rich peasants, were the enemies, and had their whole lifestyle, personalities
and social status modified and transformed, or fled the country, or were
simply killed. Being a capitalist, or in any way remotely connected with
capitalists, was one of the worst things to be in the CR. The greatest
ideological crimes of Liu Shaoqi and Deng Xiaoping, the number one and
two enemies of this period, was the way in which their policies could be
construed as capitalist. The results of pure Maoist policies was the effective

bankrupting of the Chinese system, a situation made all the more painful by that fact that overseas Chinese in places as far as the US, Singapore, Malaysia and Indonesia were showing the first real hints of their awesome entrepreneurial ability and energy. As William Van Kemenade pointed out in *China, Hong Kong, Taiwan Inc.*, if the overseas Chinese populations were put together (they number about 50 million) they would make up a country with way and afar the highest GDP per head in the world.[5] In the motherland, Mainland PRC., however, the Maoist straightjacket had scuppered this.

In the 1980s, when things first eased up, visiting business people could hunt out partners with 'export-import' powers, authorized to trade with foreign currency. But they too were state run entities, and interaction with them involved the same bureaucratic games as with the old SOEs. Business meant patient engagement with myriad, labyrinthine departments. Deals could be kicked from one end of these organizations to the other, with no sense of urgency or time. And those that did emerge successful were as much the result of luck as science.

In the New PRC, in theory one can do business much more easily. Everyone, in fact, wants to do business with you. It is the hobby, passion and lifeblood of the times. Delegations abroad are more often than not focussed on trade promotion. The last thing even the highest level Chinese politician wants to do in front of a foreign audience is spell out the scholastic intricacies of the One China policy, or, even more terrifying, start defending the PRC's human rights record. It's business for breakfast, lunch and dinner.

In fact, the storyline of the booming PRC has been running for longer than people remember. In 1993, Paul Theroux in an *Observer* supplement waxed lyrical about the 'current boom' in the PRC. In the 1980s, it seemed like every investor and foreign brand was piling in. Pierre Cardin opened a restaurant and clothes shops in Beijing. Journalist Orville Schell wrote the first of several breathless accounts of the amazing things that Chinese companies were doing.[6] Two decades later, the only thing that has changed is the size of the figures talked about. Millions have been superseded by hundreds of millions, and now billions. People sniff at Yuan billionaires. The real thing is dollar, or sterling. '*Yuan* is only good for wiping your arse', as an eloquent taxi driver once commented to me on the journey from the airport into Beijing (a site of so many memorable initial and continuing impressions of China. Perhaps no single piece of road has been the location for so much miscommunication).

---

5   *China, Hong Kong, Taiwan, Inc.: The Dynamics of a New Empire* New York 1998.
6   For an example, see *To Get Rich is Glorious: China in the 1980s*, New York 1986.

More people are involved in this great game than ever before. More people knowingly sit in increasingly opulent hotel lobbies, grandly discoursing on the fact that, of course, everyone now knows it is nonsense to talk about the idea that if every Chinaman buys your product, you'll be a multi-billionaire by the end of the night. We're here for a real deal now. But as Studwell and others have shown, tracking down the ones that really do business that delivers the same profits and performance as in other markets proves surprisingly difficult. In fact, tracking down any kind of cool, factual description of what people are doing proves hard. Companies seem in a state of perpetual preparation, about to sign, getting ready to sign, working on the final person in the relationship labyrinth. And any suggestion that they might just be very similar to the business people from the years before living in a state of constant preparedness for contracts that never came, or when they came proved far less than expected, is viewed as distasteful and inappropriate cynicism. This is not to say that a lot of people aren't doing proper business in China. It's just that they seem to talk about it in a totally different way to anywhere else.

It's the Story, Stupid

When people engage with the Chinese economy, they engage with a story. It is perhaps the most deeply loved myth of redemption and reversed fortunes existing in the modern world. Look at the primitive, downtrodden Chinese under the cudgel, the story goes. See how they suffered and fell behind. But then, in 1978, the hero of the tale, Deng Xiaoping, returned from the political graveyard for the third time (the third coming is a particularly neat part of the tale). Against all the odds, the Chinese bit by bit recover from their collective nervous breakdown suffered during the CR. They start the standing up they promised themselves they would do in 1949. They start the standing up Napoleon warned they would do two hundred years before.

In the 1980s and 1990s there were, of course, parts of this story that were at times both embarrassing and unfortunate. The Chinese did not move towards becoming a democracy, even when other countries, like the former USSR, did. Moments of painful hope like the events leading up to 4 June 1989 only resulted in bitter disappointment afterwards when it was revealed that there were parts of this reform process that were non-negotiable. Those warm meetings and that great mood music that business people from outside heard in the 1980s was abruptly curtailed by the irrefutable proof (what was that guy standing before the tank in Tiananmen Square in that iconic image doing?) that in the end, the old Maoist instincts that power grew from the end of gun still persisted.

But as the 1990s wore on, for outsiders the story was framed more subtly. Sure, economic opening up had not delivered the sort of political reforms that had been expected. The creation of what looked like an educated, articulate, successful middle class did not mean there were hordes of new wealthy standing in the streets demanding that their economic power be met with some political power. But in the long term, this was the only possible route. Bit by bit, the PRC would evolve into a Western style democracy. Such analysts would praise the village democracy movement, and the signs of the coming of participatory local politics. They would mull over the legal reforms, the raft of changes to the constitution and the legislation, and the words of senior leaders that democracy was in the post, and that this and this alone was the only way to preserve stability in the PRC.

And who could really blame the Chinese for taking this route? The USSR from being the poster boy of democratic reform had transformed into a world-class basket case, splitting up into various countries, some of which (the euphoniously named 'Stans' in particular) became brand leaders in gross human rights violations, corruption and political nepotism. Say what you like, but to the average Chinese looking at the lot of the Russians post the Gorbachev reforms, Democracy had not delivered. Indeed the global love-in with democracy had, by the mid 2000s, been greatly compromised by the fact that its chief proponents, Messrs Blair and Bush, had an unfortunate proclivity to invade other countries, set up ramshackle systems, and pass fiercely undemocratic looking legislations under the comfort blanket of counter terrorism in their home countries. The Chinese cadre's snort at the limitations of Western style democracy led more and more visitors to believe they were onto something and that in fact, Chinese democracy, like Microsoft Word XP, was on the way and would be a greatly improved version of the tired charades being delivered in the West. Democracy with Chinese characteristics seemed a dead certainty, just as socialism with Chinese characteristics had been an accepted part of the Western intellectual furniture for so long.

In 2007, the buy-in to these narratives of the Chinese economy is complete. We are now officially in a position where both for insiders and outsiders, not believing in the power and potential of the Chinese economy and the language of Chinese economism is regarded as simply madness. But the shadow of the State, and the State's involvement in the PRC and it's functioning, carries on raising all sorts of odd questions. All land in the PRC is, after all, owned by the State. So the great private enterprise you have built up is, in the end, located on land that you do not have the right to hold the freehold on even if you wanted to. Your bidding for contracts above a certain value relies on the support of the State. Your ability to transfer money into and out of China relies on the agreement of the Chinese State – and is curtailed by the current inconvertibility of the Chinese currency. The State is your best friend, and your worst enemy. Treated well it can make you rich and powerful. Treated badly it can plunge you into the eighteenth circle of hell. The Chinese State taketh, and the Chinese State giveth. All power to the Chinese State.

Tales of Those Who Went Before

Those coming to work in the new Chinese economy need to look a little at the tales of those who went before them before becoming too wrapped up in the great theatre they are about to walk into. Tim Clissold's *Mr China* is a finely told tale of a man with money, and some knowledge of China, who still manages to see every trick in the book played on him. Bring your intellectual property here, a partner will say. And then the next day set up a factory only a hundred yards away duplicating your product, producing it more cheaply and mopping your market up. Sign a contract with us, a credible looking local business partner will announce. And before the ink is dry, on the totally sincere pretext that the conditions have changes, and so therefore has the contract, whisk your investment off to a place you will never be able to find it (usually abroad). We'll show you everything, you can trust us, a company will say. Until you find out that the people you thought were running the show weren't in fact running it at all, and that the accounts and documents they showed you were all false, and that the real accounts or documents either don't exist, or are locked away in someone's head, and will never be known to you.[7]

Both sides are now committed to that story mentioned above. The story has been written over the last 20 years, of the Chinese economy. Running like Agatha Christie's *The Mousetrap*, it still packs them in every week, to hear the tale of this great marvel. Chinese themselves live this story and breathe in the theatre and excitement it provides. Parts of the story might contain elements of truth. But to those who look long and hard at the particulars, there are always these nagging doubts that it doesn't all quite add up. The statistics, for instance, with their gaping holes. Or the lack of transparency that means that it is difficult to work out what is going on in any company or organization. The Chinese have invented some of the most fantastically

---

7   Tim Clissold, *Mr China*, London 2004.

complicated company structures on the planet. Maybe in the end, all that really matters is the story. If we didn't have the story, what would we have? In the twenty-first century, while the US spreads its particular depleted form of democratic enlightenment via stealth bombs and Wal-Mart, and Europe can barely agree on a common document to run its affairs, paradoxically the 'ancient' 5,000 year old civilization of China is offering at least some kind of future, by rebranding and repositioning itself.

The Air We Breathe, the Earth We Live On

So powerful is this story of the economy and of economism, that the main victim, the Chinese environment, has been forgotten till the last few years. Pan Yue, head of the State Environmental Protection Agency, has radically declared that in fact the PRC's economic growth over the last two decades has not been a success story at all. What has happened is that Chinese companies have clocked up double digit growth at the expense of trashing the environment, cut costs by leaving out critical environmental protection measures and that the overall price of putting this right in the next decades will more than mop up the money that the PRC has made in the last 30 years.

The impact of the PRC's commercial development on its environment is clear to see everywhere, including from outer space! The Gobi desert is now larger, because of the process of desertification that has been going on for half a century. Beijing is cursed by increasingly bad sandstorms each spring, blighting the traditionally pleasant weather then. Cities like Lanzhou in Gansu and Xian in Shaanxi, home of the terracotta warriors, suffer thick polluted fogs and falls of coal dust that coat the outside and inside of things (including the human body). In some parts of the PRC, over 70 per cent of water is undrinkable. The recent flow of pollution from Russia into Harbin in Northern PRC might be taken by some as nothing more than rough justice – an outsider for once returning to the PRC what it produces in such abundance itself.

At the start of the Opening Up reforms in the early 1980s, the imperative was simply on developing quickly. Like in the Great Leap Forward of the 1950s, factories were built with next to no environmental protection measures. Forests were flattened, buildings flung up, all with little, if any, planning. The reward, after 20 years, is to have 16 of the world's 20 most polluted cities. Respiratory diseases floor the PRC's population in winter, and they suffer increasingly frequent floods and heat waves in the summer. The campaign to plant a billion trees around Beijing before 2008 was felled by the simple fact that there was not enough water to sustain them and many died. Air conditioning in most urban new housings, increasing car usage and massive demands on the environment are likely to increase the problems before they get better – if they can. All of this in the name of economic development. Tellingly, only in the last few years has the PRC even talked about sustainable development. Most of its activities in the 1980s and 1990s were clearly not sustainable, and as Pan Yue said, will take enormous effort, resources, and willpower to put right – if, indeed, they even can.

In the twenty-first century, then, the PRC's environment has become our environment. Already acid rain over the US is being blamed partly on the effect of the Chinese influence on the global environment. If there is one area where we should, and must, collaborate it is addressing this crisis immediately, through technology share, political support and investment. As a symbol of the united world we live in, and of the way one country's problems frequently, and in the environment inevitably, becomes others', this takes top priority. If we can't work together here, then our talk of working as one in other areas is, and will only ever be, mere words.

CHAPTER TEN:
CHINESE CHARACTERS

The question will usually rise quite soon into a conversation with those deep into the second phase of their encounter as outsiders with the PRC. Ok, even the most sympathetic listener will respond, you don't like the pollution, the crowding, the food is starting to wear you down, the bureaucracy and lack of transparency are obviously taking their toll. You're fed up with so many things, why on earth are you still here? And the answer, invariably, will come back, because of the people.

China's landscape and its historical artefacts – what museum curators call material culture – have been compromised and degraded. Most Chinese cities have lost what little charm and elegance they may ever have had in a wave of modernization, so that ceramic tiles and blue tinted glass reign supreme from one end of the country to the other. The few cities with any real distinctness left – Pingyao, in north China, or Suzhou with its walled gardens, or Lhasa, with its Medieval style pageant on the rooftop of the world – are all enclaves under siege from the waves of tourists and 'conservationists' who, however, well meaning, frequently literally rebuild and remake the historical treasure they are meant to preserve.

The treatment of the physical terrain, as I argued at the end of the last chapter, is deeply problematic in the PRC. But in fact, as Judith Shapiro shows in her book about China's environment, this is not surprising.[1] The typical understanding of Chinese culture is one final paradox – that this is a place where the human is celebrated over the non-human, the natural world. Mao himself would declare, in his writing and his own activity, that nature was there to be tamed and subsumed, by human effort. Massive public campaigns were waged to eradicate sparrows, destroy forests, redirect rivers and create man-made dams. The world was there to write a human

---

1   Judith Shapiro, *Mao's War Against Nature: Politics and the Environment in Revolutionary China*, Cambridge 2001.

signature across. And this in a culture that at the same time contained so much classical art that placed nature above and over man.

For students of human behaviour, the PRC is a rich arena for observation. It is a culture that celebrates the importance of relations between people – and allows these to operate on a level that is hardly ever obvious. There is no clear, rigid hierarchy as there is in Japan, where verb forms indicate power relations in spoken speech. Nor is the relation between genders that straightforward – the PRC and its preceding dynasties have enjoyed (if that is the right word) some of the most formidable female figures in history. While one can put up good arguments for it being a place where age barriers are respected, there are aberrations like the CR, where respect for age was thrown to the wind. It is a place that could be called conservative, but has experienced radical revolutions every few decades – a place where the family seems to offer the basic network, but where, as one recent observer has noted, people are capable of acting with breathtaking selfishness, living away from their partners and children in a way that Westerners frequently find harsh and baffling.

The only way to understand Chinese people, it would seem, is to try to describe different types, and see what patterns emerge. Broad descriptions like the one Takeo Doi produced about Japan don't work in the PRC, or at least no one has cracked it so far.[2] At best there are complicated academic studies of the myriad groups that constitute parts of the great pageant that is Chinese society now. The only rule that seems to work is that no rules really work. Chinese people just are what they are. But in this chapter, I want to sketch out some of the sort of character types that you might come across in the journey across the human geography of the PRC today and the actors who will be performing in the tale that unfolds over the next two decades.

The Cadre

He sits behind his desk in a room about the same size as the building you have just had to walk through to reach his door. There are bookcases behind, and armchairs arranged in a rectangle around a large carpet. He stands up only at the very last moment, after you have made your journey across the floor, holding out his hand almost tentatively, looking past you slightly distracted by the queue of people who have walked into the room behind you, only half of whom you know. His handshake is brisk, businesslike. You notice his perfectly arranged black hair, his neat suit, and

2   *The Anatomy of Dependence,* Tokyo 1971.

the orderly pile of papers on his desk. He greets everyone else with the same briskness, and you all sit down. There is an uncomfortable silence. 'Who's going to speak first?', he says, staring round him. You say a few words, but just as you are getting into your stride, a mobile phone rings, and the cadre pulls a small, trendy set from his pocket, and answers it, almost oblivious now to the dozen or so people in the room, forced to eavesdrop on his conversation. When he attends to you all again, he has the same distracted air, and after your introit he responds with words you have heard a hundred times before, courteous, formal, welcoming words, devoid of any real meaning, read from the great hymn sheet, the collective discourse of cadres the length and breadth of the land.

The Chinese cadre occupies a permanent but somewhat ambiguous place in the theatre of contemporary PRC. Those new to the PRC are rightly surprised by this. Surely, they feel, now that the PRC has changed to market socialism, this sort of figure should have receded into the background. But like all great soap operas and actors, the Chinese cadre has evolved and developed. The old style character dressed in a Sun Yatsen suit, with large framed classes and a permanent smile, omnipresent in photos of delegation visits to China from 1949 to the 1980s, has faded away. Now the cadre dresses in well cut western style suits, is mostly male, with dyed black hair if over 50, sometimes sporting a Rolex watch and branded clothes, and, within a certain allowable range, loudly declaring their power through the signifiers available in the PRC – chauffeur driven cars, nice housing. Nothing too explicit or ostentatious – that would stray into the territory of corruption and break the unwritten rules. But a sign in their manner and their air of being close to the elixir of power, and people who, of course, are easy and good to keep on ones side and hell if their paths are ever crossed.

However obvious it might seem, the key thing about cadres is that they are Party members. They belong to the clan. And outsiders must remember that the institution they belong too, so often pooh-poohed and sidelined, still has its hands on all the main levers of power in the Chinese universe. Remember that the Party has 60 million members, exceeding the population of most countries. And that membership of it carries benefits that, however undefinable, are still worth the burdens of applying to join. Party members are different to other people. Like being a Catholic or a Muslim, membership is a statement of some sort of belief, though not necessarily ideological commitment to Marxism-Leninism. Just an adherence to certain beliefs about the importance of power, the need for a unified power source, and the ways in which that power should be exercised. Party members may know that they work in a world where the police, army and law courts are all semi-functional, and that there might be problems with this – but the imperatives of maintaining Party power make that all OK. And they inherit a revolutionary tradition fathered by the immortals, from Mao Zedong onwards. Whatever disasters they inflicted on the Chinese people and the state they built up, in the end there is the need for deeper allegiance to them, no matter what the historians might throw up. The Party's appeal is visceral and membership as much emotional as pragmatic in its benefits.

The Chinese cadre in 2007 is hamstrung by the very public realization that the old discourse they could channel into, spouting Marxist-Leninist truths, is dead. Marx, in particular, may well be the most acute critic capitalism ever had and his analytic deconstruction of the free market as much needed now as it ever was, but there are few believers in him as a supplier of ideological dogma, and of truth through dialectics. Chinese society has embraced the full rigours of capitalist excess, and declares it in the landscape, in the behaviour of people, and in the economic imperatives of each of the five year plans. Cadres are no longer channels by which the revealed truths of Marxism can be relayed via Maoist purification. They are, in fact, keyholders, administrators and functionaries within the great system to maintain the material hold of the Party on power. As such, their role is both one of controlling, limiting and supplying boundaries that they must then vigilantly guard. This ironically applies less to what Cadres do, than to what they say and what they don't say. Cadres can partake of the same fleshly glories of the new Chinese theatre as their fellow countrymen who have leapt into the sea of the private sector. They can, up to a point, moan about the same problems that others do, and even admit mistakes in the Party. They can laugh loudly when you josh with them about the importance of Marxist-Leninist class struggle, their sounds of mirth an open admission that this adherence to ideology exists only on the level of language. But they won't say that the Party should allow multi-Party elections, they definitely won't say that Taiwan should be allowed independence (or Tibet, or Xinjiang). In fact, they will be fervent nationalists.

The loosening up of the Chinese economy, with many SOEs shifted over to the private sector and the break down of much bureaucratic control of industry in the PRC, gives outsiders the impression that, much like in the West, there are reasonably well defined lines between the state and the private sector. But the waiting rooms of commercial sections of the foreign embassies in Beijing are full of people with tales of woe about the trouble that local government officials can cause companies and joint ventures, that catch their eye and for some reason irritate them. Cadres can be sensitive and jealous of their power, even all the more so as it is diminishing. Failure to keep them informed might be a source of friction, if only because it does not accord them enough face. But, more dangerously, they may have interests and links into the so-called private sector that would surprise and confuse outsiders like partial ownership of areas that they regulate, or family links that are not visible on first encounter. And maybe too, the setting up of a sleek, lean JV (Joint Venture) in a specific area threatens local industries, and calls to the fore a sense of localized patriotism that means the cadre uses all the power in their dark armoury to push you away.

And cadres in China, as Joe Studwell pointed out, like bureaucrats anywhere, have a very specific attitude. To them, the game is not about simply quantifiable things like profit and loss, or delivering shareholder value. The outcomes are more complicated than that. The sorts of incentives that push along those in the great worlds of commerce or private enterprise do not exist in the same way to them. The sense of urgency and anxiety to push on to the closure of the next deal that pervades business people's lives is something they find both amusing and incomprehensible. And over the last two decades they have developed a system where this difference in attitude can itself become a useful bargaining chip. To visiting business people, time is money. To help their comrades in the private sector, officials can throw up any number of regulatory or administrative barriers that stall deals. The Chinese company director opposite you will participate in your sense of frustration as much as you, but tell you that there is nothing he can do – the decision has been pushed into some area of local government. As time wears on, you wear down. Just to nail any deal at all you offer far more than you ever thought you would till the mysterious zones of the bureaucracy you were waiting to hear from start making favourable noises.

So cadres should never be underestimated. Like Priests and Ministers of Religion in the West, they have powers and influences that can be critical at most of the crucial junctures of life in the PRC. With a wave of their hand, they can make your day by foregoing the need for a part of an impossibly long process to usher your JV into existence, and with another wave throw you into jeopardy and hell by demanding some final piece of paper or document. They may be harder to spot that they used to be, huddled round the edges. But like an opera without the chorus or an orchestra without the banks of strings, the PRC as it is now would not be the PRC without them. And that is why, of all the beasts one meets in the Chinese jungle, they still rank as servants of the kings.

The Chinese Miss

Her energy and forthrightness takes you back. First up, she smiles knowingly when you open your mouth, like she knows what you are about to say even before you've said it. She might be 21, but she has the air about her of an expert on everything she says. And she slightly knocks you off your stride when she touches your arm, sits very close to you and now and then brushes against you. You don't even bother to try to speak Chinese to her, even though, while her English is excellent, there is something irritating and unnatural about her manner of delivery. It's only when she declares that, of course, foreigners need to do more to understand the Chinese way of thinking that you mischievously suggest that maybe the 'Chinese way of thinking' is a myth in its own right. A massive red herring like the 'Asian values' nonsense that was kicked up by the Singaporean leader, Lee Kuan Yew in the mid 1990s. For the first time she looks a little uncertain. But before long, she is declaring vehemently that connections, connections and only connections are all that matters in the PRC and then drops you a few names of people she has contact with, through, of course, her parents.

It's a true story, one not that well known in the PRC, but recorded in black and white in the transcripts of Richard Nixon's 1972 visit.[3] A feeble Mao, sitting on the worn and homely sofas with their doily arm covers in his spectacular scholarly eyrie in the Zhongnanhai Compound in Beijing, was wowing Nixon and his entourage. Mao airily declared that it would be an easy thing to topple America. How, asked the dazzled Nixon. Just send over ten thousand Chinese women, Mao responded. That would sort the place out in a couple of years. An acerbic footnote in the book comments that at this time Mao was experiencing particular problems with his wife Jiang Qing who had been kept neatly in the shadows till the CR, but then come into her own as one of the radical leadership. Jiang Qing, while widely loathed these days, still elicits appalled admiration from some for the fact that she was one of the few powerful women in the first 40 years of the PRC and for that reason and that alone offered one of the few role models.

Mao's comment and indeed his attitude towards women generally, were representative of the ambiguous way in which women have been viewed in Chinese society. Honoured in his immortal tribute that 'women held up half the sky', they have also had to labour under almost impossible strictures for the last half a century. The current generation of young Chinese women,

---

3   William Burr (ed) : *Kissinger Transcripts: The Top Secret Talks With Beijing And Moscow*, New York 1999.

while freer than any of those preceding them, might sometimes look and sound, like they are caught between a rock and a hard place – with demands on them to be mothers, sex objects and business people. And there is, in Chinese society, more than its fare share of sexual stereotyping.

In contemporary PRC the number of women occupying high positions is few and far between. There is the redoubtable Wu Yi, now Vice Premier, a woman of formidable energy and stamina, who, it is rumoured, once had the previous President of China Yang Shangkun fall on his knees and declare undying love to her only to be slapped round the face and called a fool. The former Education Minister Chen Zhili was, so the rumour mill claimed, a favourite of the then President Jiang Zemin. It seemed that any woman who had political ambitions in the PRC had to get used to the fundamental occupational hazard that their main claim to power would be connections with some more powerful male. In fact, Chinese political culture is as full as innuendo and whispered slurry about the main players as any other – but made all the more salacious because it cannot be aired in the media, or openly discussed.

The status of women has been affected by one phenomenon unique to the PRC. Because of the vagaries of the one child system, and the general desire in the countryside to give birth to boy, illegal but still widely practiced birth control methods have led to a significant gender imbalance in favour of men. In the PRC now there are up to 50 million more men than women. This has spawned the phenomenon of rural men needing to literally kidnap brides because of the lack of suitable potential wives locally. But it has also meant that ironically, women, being in the minority, are able to be far choosier about their potential partners.

Not that their new found powers are immediately visible. Red ribbon cutting ceremonies, or seminars, or delegations abroad tend to still be populated mostly by men. The women that come along, more times than not, are translators, or lower officials. The Chinese diplomatic service is even worse than the British one in appointing female ambassadors. In public events, most of the time women are decorative – the ones wearing the slit *qipao* dresses and holding the scissors before the VIPs slice through the red ribbon and declare whatever it is they are celebrating.

But in Beijing and Shanghai and other urban centres, there is a new generation of women – women employed by the thousands of foreign companies now based there, able to speak good English, dressed in designer clothes and driving their own cars. Like the generation of independent Japanese women who grew into themselves during the economic miracle in the 1970s and 1980s, this group has plenty of expendable income. They are in no great hurry to have children, or tie themselves down and are independent minded. No wrapping Chinese dumplings in the cramped work-unit supplied kitchen for them. These are the customers of the new sexy lingerie shops popping up in Beijing, Shanghai and other urban centres now – women every bit as demanding and sophisticated in their tastes and expectations as their western counterparts. And they don't suffer half as gladly and silently as their immediate precursors. Despite a huge social stigma, the divorce rate in the PRC is creeping up as high and as fast as the decadent western societies the PRC once so puritanically cast itself in opposition too. And divorce is extremely simple – a day- long bureaucratic exercise without even the pauses and longueurs that are put up in most Western countries.

Those who visit the PRC or are based there for any length of time become very familiar with this segment of the population. Most companies or organizations tend to have quite a few good examples. Like the world over, women prove themselves to be more competent or at least engaged linguists than men and so for the foreigners restricted to English, these are usually the points of contact and entry. Part of the package of being a Little Chinese Miss these days seems to be the absolute need to speak good English. English is the signifier of internationalization and is part of the package of being a cosmopolitan, urbane, sophisticated young Chinese woman.

And it has to be said that there is a chemical equation, almost, that creates near perfect arrogance in some of the more extreme samples of this character type. Combine the effects of the one child policy (very spoilt children), education abroad (making young Chinese even more effective promoters of the less acceptable aspects of their society), and the general breakneck materialism of Chinese contemporary society, where haves are almost worshipped, and have-nots can go to the wall, and one ends up with individuals who can come across, in their mid twenties, as both patronising, condescending, arrogant and, at the same time, utterly unaware of the impact of their behaviour on those around them. To them, in fact, you are just lucky to be able to walk for a few moments in their reflected glory.

One should, after all, spare a thought for young men in contemporary Chinese society. Fighting to find a partner in a dwindling pool of females, they have to then see the more and more common sight of a lot of their potential wives hook up with the vast band of foreigners now knocking about. They have to enter certain economic bands to even have a chance to compete in this game, delivering a package of luxury houses, cars, money, branded goods – all of it to demonstrate that in the currency of this new world they are 'players' and merit the final sign of success – a tamed, satisfied, high quality wife! Not surprisingly, for any onlooker, relationships in the PRC seem as frayed, vulnerable, and based on wishful thinking and mutual deception as any other developed society. In this area, too, the PRC has more than caught up with the West!!

The Chinese Intellectual

A man of 50 or so in a black polo neck jumper. A smoker, with wary eyes, and sensuous lips. A slightly harried look about him, and a prickliness which comes to the surface as soon as you sit down, and he pats on the book on the table in front of him and asks why it is that you didn't ever bother to reply to that email he sent you months before. After all, he says, although he knows his English is not that good, just a two or three word reply would have been enough. It gives him a chance to practice his English. And in any case, going through the intermediary who had introduced you both is no longer necessary. You are friends now, aren't you? You can have direct contact. No need to stand on ceremony. Then he pushes the essay that you had written and had translated into Chinese towards you. You can see that it is covered with his comments and suggestions. Well, he says, this is a good essay, it introduces Chinese to Western ideas and ways of thinking. But the arrangement of it, that needs to be changed so that, he pauses, looks at you hard, well, so that it suits our Chinese way of thinking better. And when you start to argue that surely the logic should be the same, in either Chinese or English, he looks vaguely affronted and irritated. The friend with you tells you after the meeting, I guess he is just not used to having someone dissent. He's a Chinese intellectual. He's used to speaking and having others listen. He's not used to someone butting in.

The Chinese intellectual deserves a special place in our pantheon. To have a social class so overtly called intellectuals in the first place might strike westerners as rather quaint. Those that declare themselves openly to be intellectuals in countries like the UK tend to run the hazard of being regarded a little like other socially excluded groups – paedophiles, for instance, or criminals – people who are engaged in something shameful and covert, and whose best policy should simply be to maintain silence about their dirty little secret.

The Maoist classification of Chinese society, however, embedded the idea very early on that there was a discreet group of people who were engaged in mental activity, and these were the intellectuals. This covered anyone from university lecturers, high school and primary school teachers, students, and those who were engaged in the purer intellectual pursuits – writers, artists, scientists and journalists. Such a diverse group were tarred almost from the start in the PRC as being riddled with unreliability and mental pollution. Given a chance, famously, to air their grievances about the new system in the Hundred Flowers campaign of 1957, they rewarded Mao and his government with an avalanche of complaints and criticisms, before being silenced by a brutal purge. Dai Qing, a long established Chinese writer, called this the first of many shameful capitulations by the intellectual class. Instead of showing any unity, according to her account, they engaged in a vicious bout of mutual recriminations and betrayals, vying with each other to display their real loyalty to the regime in selling others. There were courageous isolated exceptions. Hu Feng, for instance, the former protégé of the great writer Lu Xun, was rewarded for his mild criticism by being incarcerated for over two decades. But others were to be less hard-headed – or foolish, depending on how you view things. A goodly dose of self-criticism, and some well targeted denunciations of others was usually enough to keep body and soul together, while the Chinese state moved its targets on to other areas.

The early sixties were preoccupied with grappling with the fallout from the economic folly of the Great Leap Forward. Mao withdrew from active political life, and left the country in the capable hands of Liu Shaoqi and Deng Xiaoping, who, while they were not enamoured of the intellectuals, at least did not actively seek fights with them. The CR, of course, changed all that, marking the period of all-out conflict with the PRC's intelligentsia, pushing some of them down to concentration camps (going under the name of Cadre Schools) and driving others at best to internal exile and at very worst to death. Suicide, institutionalized in Chinese culture as the honourable response by intellectuals to tyranny on the death of the great poet Qu Yuan two thousand years before, became the exit of choice for some of the country's finest writers and artists, among them writer Lao She and playwright and politician, Wu Han. Thousands of less well known, but equally worthy individuals died, either at their own hands, or by others.

In the aftermath of the CR, the celebration of the Four Modernizations (Science, Industry, Agriculture and Defence) meant that the PRC now needed those most broadly branded as intellectuals more than ever. Stopping university lessons for several years had not helped things, nor had alienating and disenfranchising so many of the most gifted and intelligent people. Once more, the Party tried to square the age-old circle – creating politically reliable, but intellectually capable and inquisitive individuals. There were some very nasty hiccoughs along this process – the most damaging being the events of 1989, where students were the main participants.

The Chinese intellectual, like the Chinese politician, in many ways his natural enemy, can be classified into a number of generations. The very earliest, educated in the 1940s and 1950s, were to enjoy the benefits of an oddly more open and cosmopolitan environment than those that followed them, frequently able to speak Russian, often English, beneficiaries (at least if they had been educated in the 1940s) of the foreign missionary run schools in some of the main Chinese cities. The second generation of Chinese intellectuals, educated in the 1960s and 1970s, are those that are in senior positions in universities and other areas of activity today. These carry the scars of the great close down from the CR, and of the turbulent campaigns waged then. But they also enjoyed the somewhat ambiguous benefit of a period when literally any ideas or suggestions were given airing space – a paradox of the CR discussed in Chapter 4. The intellectuals from this period are, perhaps with some good reason, able to lecture those after them on the greater toughness and independence of their thought because of the extraordinary period in which they grew up.

Intellectuals afterwards have had the easiest run. Many have been able to go abroad to be educated (though in the 1980s, a famously high proportion of those who first went to the US to study on behalf of the motherland, never actually came back). They are more cosmopolitan, mostly able to speak foreign languages, and have had good access, especially through the Internet, to ideas from outside, though with certain clear restrictions.

But a contemporary, young Chinese intellectual has to live with one huge contradiction. They are part of one of the world's great intellectual traditions, a culture that produced the sort of scientific achievements documented and celebrated in Joseph Needham's monumental (and ongoing, despite Needham's own death in 1995) *Science and Civilisation in China*. They are the inheritors of one of the world's greatest bodies of literature, including works that date back three thousand years, and embrace some of the greatest poetry ever written in any language. In the arenas of material culture, too, China through the previous dynasties ranks as one of the world's greatest traditions.

And yet the world in which Chinese intellectuals operate now is one that largely relegates, or ignores, these achievements and certainly places a highly ambiguous value on intellectual achievement and effort. There is a mocking saying, popular in the mid 1990s, but now so wired into Chinese perceptions as to hardly need saying, that once one gets a doctorate one is then truly qualified to be poor! University teachers and researchers are amongst the most poorly paid, and almost all of them are engaged in moonlighting.

To be a Chinese intellectual, too, remains high-risk. Simply doing business means that, barring flagrant corruption, your Achilles's heels are limited. But intellectuals, in their adventures of articulation and expression, are prone to stray into the shady area where suddenly they find they have committed ideological crimes. Historians and political scientists, in particular, find that once they discuss subjects closer to home they have to exercise enormous caution. The net result is that, beyond the most dire party-line accounts or popularist potboilers, serious scholarship in Chinese on the CR has almost ceased and become the sole province either of outside scholars or Chinese with the luxury of operating from abroad.

Chinese society has become as dumbed down as any other, with a deluge of magazines, films and TV programmes with the most limited production values and precious little to say. The worship of material success in fact means that, more often than not, people who are seen as doing well are never particularly judged on their intelligence, but on their business instinct – their ability to make money. This means that while Chinese intellectuals might declare their support for the finer things, they are doing so to a dwindling audience. The rest have all scurried off following the great god Mammon. And as a Chinese business advisor I was discussing this with said, it's no good trying to reach Chinese entrepreneurs through books and magazines. They just don't read them. All they do is make money.

Not that Chinese intellectuals themselves cannot transform into the most ruthless, unappealing capitalists. Ten years ago I had a particularly nasty encounter with a university professor who heard about my interest in the CR and let it be known he had a good collection of pamphlets from that time. Of course, it was never going to be anything as crude and vulgar as suggesting he might want to part with them for money, but that was the well understood sub-text. Mr Wang, if we can call him that, invited me round to his well appointed apartment in the university and let me look through the books. It was, indeed, good stuff. But most of the time he was distracting me by saying that of course, this rubbish was of no real interest to anyone and the last thought on his mind was to try and part with it. It was just of personal interest to him.

Then the moment of embarrassment came. I'd like to buy them, I said. He droned on at even greater length about the fact that it would be an offence to sell such a good man as I such paltry rubbish. I gave up on getting anything as silly as a specific starting price out of him, and proposed 50 pounds. This seemed pretty generous at a time when the average monthly wage was about that. The man's well lived-in face froze. Well, no, I don't think that will do at all, he said, sharply. Then the smile returned and the oily, smooth manner. I have already had offers from American friends, of 700 to 800 dollars, he said.

I stood dumbstruck. But that's hard to understand, I said, at last, these are Chinese language books, there can't be more than a handful of people in the world with any interest in them now, a Chinese person wouldn't even pay you 1 per cent of that. Maybe so, the teacher said, with towering certainty. And I realized that we had crossed a line and that he couldn't possibly back down from his crazy lie about being able to flog them for over ten times what I was willing to pay. I realized the deal was dead. 'That's the trouble with intellectuals when they try to do business', a friend wearily commented, 'they tend to go silly and ask for daft sums'.

Intellectuals, with their notional social prestige and their threatened place, can therefore come across as being like an endangered species, prickly, slightly uncertain, trying to operate in an environment where they are no longer sure of the rules, easy to take offence. They come across as feeling like they are the guardians of something very important in Chinese culture, though they don't quite know what. It is perhaps a sense of elitism, and of power based on the refined knowledge of the mandarin class, their historical predecessors, which, of course, was challenged and overturned in 1949. The new elite can better be described as a peasant elite (Mao is sometimes referred to as the Peasant emperor, despite the fact he came from a reasonably wealthy background and probably qualified as an intellectual in his own right). Intellectuals almost seem to have to apologize for their being who they are. These days, in fact, they have to adopt all the disguises and self-obfuscation as their fellow intellectuals abroad. And the first rule of this is, unless you do it really really well, it is best not to do it at all, and pretend you are like everyone else. And in the case of the PRC, that means carry on doing as much as you can to make lots and lots of money.

The New Elite – Entrepreneurs

He sits in his hotel room, in one of the mini presidential suites, with a stranger you've never seen before, but who you assume, when you sit down in the settee at the other end of the room, is either his driver or his assistant – one of the many. You notice he seems to be wearing a Burberry jacket, and Church shoes. He has three mobiles lined up on the table in front of him, which chime together and which he answers with a curt 'Yes, who is it' and then barks instructions and closes them without any further courtesies. And then he sits back and looks at you, and waits for you to speak. That is what you have been told to expect. This is a man, people say, who really knows how to keep cadres happy. A man who has built up a small private empire, all his own, but kept the right side of the leadership. He knows what to look for in the people he deals with – greed, lust, anger, vanity. But because you are slightly out of any of these boxes, you sense a tentativeness about his approach to you and a slight lack of self-assurance. Most of his conversation is about his trips abroad. He has been to more countries than you and tells you that his passport is now full up with visas. And then he moves on to tell you about the million yuan he lost gambling in Hong Kong. But that is small beer. He made it up the night afterwards. You remember playing mahjong with him and trust that his gambling instincts are good, because on that one occasion you saw him wipe the board with an experienced player opposite you. All the time you are talking, you are acutely aware of the stories you have heard about his temper the way people fear him back in his hometown and about the string of mistresses he has. You can't quite reconcile that with the diffident slightly cowed figure before you – until he barks an order at the guy sitting nearby, who, despite being nearly twice his size, leaps up and acts like a timid manservant, going to fetch the car that will take you to your next appointment.

The dominant discourse in the PRC now, the great glue welding this vast creation together, is, as I argued earlier in this book, the language of economism, development and commerce. Politicians, artists, academics, all sing to this common hymn sheet. Even the disapproving have to recognize the great wave of development, that has washed not only over the landscape but into every area of their minds. The gradual actualization of the PRC's potential through its economic development has become the greatest whale in the sea of Chineseness, something no one can avoid, and even in the act of avoiding is making a statement about. Economism is in the air that the Chinese breathe, in the food they eat and the land they tread on.

And the true apostles of this language are the entrepreneurs, the businessmen and, more and more frequently now, women, who have learnt and mastered the arts of capitalism with Chinese characteristics and are now adept practitioners. They can be called many things – the new aristocracy, the new elite or the vanguard of the Chinese world takeover. People to either love or fear, depending on how you view the future of the Chinese economy, and the position of the country in the world.

In the good old bad old Maoist days, displays of status and wealth were anathema, except to the tiny minority of the truly powerful. Even they had to practice well honed routines of concealing what they really had and enjoyed behind great walls of privacy. People dressed the same, ate the same and lived in the same manner. No one wanted to stand out. The state owned everything from housing to the few vehicles that bustled along the roads with their cadre passengers. All restaurants, and hotels, and shops, were state owned, selling goods with regulated prices, and manned by state employees who were filling in the days and hours before their state-supported retirement.

These days, a whole new type of person has appeared in the Chinese firmament. From being the greatest devils in the Hades of the Chinese world, business people have emerged as the heroes of the story, the characters dragging a rejuvenated PRC right to the front of the queue in the twenty-first century. From being dumped into jail and disowned in the 1950s and 1960s, capitalists (for that is what in essence they are) are now allowed to be members of the Party. The sterling contribution of the private sector to the economy was recognized by the Party in 2003 by a bold mention in the constitution. Some more cynical observers only saw this as the Party bowing to the inevitable. With perhaps as much as 50 per cent of the Chinese growth rate being generated by the private sector now, and only 170 companies still in the state's hands, it's hard to see what else they could do. But this private/state distinction is as full of shadows as the rest of the great Chinese terrain and eminently open to dispute.

What is not disputable is the emergence of a very visible class, the new Chinese entrepreneur. They are all over the main cities now. Beijing is full of their expensive imported cars. The upper end restaurants, which seem to exist to serve uneatable food at phenomenally expensive prices – the more uneatable, the more expensive – are heaving with cool looking customers, draped in branded coats and jewellery, declaring their status over every inch of their body. And the new elite love dropping casually into their conversation the enormous amounts of money they have just needed to spend on sending their children abroad, buying another new house and setting up a company to do business more conveniently through Hong Kong.

Of course, there is a sophisticated code to all of this. Needing to bang on too much about how rich one is is a sure sign, to the other truly wealthy, that you haven't really arrived yet. The real congnoscenti study enviously the example of Li Kaishing, a genuinely wealthy man, born in China and and brought up in Hong Kong, who still maintains a life of, perhaps a little ostentatiously, great simplicity and regularly makes it onto the Forbes list of the world's top ten richest men. The Chinese excuse for themselves having so few dollar billionaires on this list is simple. The truly wealthy in the PRC would never be as stupid as to disclose their real wealth. The name of the game is to give the impression of great wealth without actually ever putting a figure on it. Horrendously complicated company structures are then created to put investigators and unwelcome intruders off the scent and leave the great wealth diffracted and extended. The impression one gets after looking at all of this is either that the truly wealthy in the PRC own half the planet – or that it is some great charade, with which one is obliged, while in the PRC, to play along.

What does a Chinese entrepreneur look like? According to Rupert Hoogewerf, long term resident of Shanghai, and compiler over the last five years of the China Rich list, the modern wealthy Chinese is more than likely to hale from the coastal province of Zhejiang (over 10 per cent of his current rich list fit this), be aged 30 to 45, be male, like wearing Rolex watches and driving BMWs. They split about fifty-fifty between those who have been educated at university, with about a quarter having been educated abroad. The old myth of the Chinese nouveau riche, peasants who have had their wealth rocket and yet can barely read, is only partially true. Like in the US and Europe, a lot of techies (people like Bill Gates or the founders of Google) are making money more because of the power of their ideas than their business sense alone.

A lot of Chinese entrepreneurs have a background in government. That gave them the connections and credibility to 'leap into the sea' and set up private businesses. One I met in Xian, had set up a fruit juice processing plant, and was now, ten years later, supplying Coca Cola and Cadbury Schweppes. With his background, he was pretty clear about how to deal with party officials. 'Just tell them that their ideas, which in fact came from you in the first place, are really good, and look after them, and they will leave you alone.' Another, in the north-east of China, had managed to build a company, which he started with some family money and a bank loan from ten people to five thousand. For him, the show of unity with the Party was the simple sign at the entrance of his factory showing his Party membership, taken out the day in 2002 when private business people were first able to join.

In fact, this interbreeding between Party and private sector people kicks off a small suspicion that they are in fact very close and show similar kinds of behaviours. As prone to talk in epic generalities as their political brothers and sisters, entrepreneurs can also, like the best of top leaders in the PRC, trot out immense, and literally meaningless statistical lists, showing phenomenal sales growths and development rates – and with your eyes closed, you could almost think one were in you of the endless congresses held by the government, celebrating a year of further magnificent successes, rather than in the boardroom of a private company.

And entrepreneurs, like officials, show the same ambiguity behind their superficial commitment to patriotic nationalism, often pushing their children with unseemly haste to set up businesses and settle abroad, sometimes ferreting their money away in offshore accounts, or seeking to set up holding companies that they then conduct their business in. A lot will vehemently declare they would rather do business with outsiders than other Chinese. 'They are too sly, too complicated, too sharp', the businessman in Shenyang rather disarmingly declared. Entrepreneurs, to outsiders, have admirable skills in dexterously manoeuvring the myriad of relationships to get their business done, while also having to be accountable to not only their business partners but to a capricious Party system that at any time might make an unwelcome appearance in their affairs.

And they also have to learn the greatest skill of all – treading the ever shifting line between the permissible and the impermissible in the great game around them – knowing who to pay off, when and how, without themselves being embroiled in a mountain of impropriety and corruption. They will have the recent high-profile case of the Fujian-based smuggler, Lai Chaixing to think over, who descended step by step into a billion dollar pit of pay-offs, bribery, sleaze and corruption before bolting along an exit route to Canada.

Zhou Enlai, it is reported, counselled people never to go into politics. It was too dangerous, cut-throat and murky. Such words must be held against the simple fact that his adopted son, Li Peng, was to carve out a career as one of China's most loathed, and largely unscathed, politicians of recent years (though it seems it is now time for a rehabilitation of sorts. For whatever Li's crimes as the front man of the crackdown on 4 June 1989, he seems to have been a back room promoter of the economic reforms that are so lauded now). Nowadays, people may feel that, as elsewhere (including the UK) for real power you shouldn't look to politics, but to business. But business people operate in a world without sentiment, with a mercurial sense of loyalty, where self-interest is always painfully close to the surface of even the most altruistic actions. And so for Chinese entrepreneurs, the terrain is as dangerous and startling as that for politicians and power players of a previous generation. No wonder they seem to so relish their trips abroad to the massage parlours of Bangkok or the Red Light streets of Amsterdam. Places to forget the giddying balancing act they need to perform every time they are back at home.

'The Rubble'

She sits beside you on the low couch. The room is dark. The businessman who has brought you here is belting out his favourite song in front of the karaoke machine. 'I love you, you love me, how happy we will be.' She is touching you, tactile, over friendly. Because the light is so bad, it is hard to tell how old she is. She is dressed in *tight black clothes, and her hair is shoulder length. 'Have you ever spoken to a foreigner before?,' you say, in Chinese. She has a heavy accent you can barely understand. `No, seen a few, never spoken to any. Lots of foreigners come to the town. But I'm not from here. I only got here a couple of months ago.' 'Where are you from?' 'The countryside.' You nod. 'Why come here? Wouldn't you prefer to be with your family?' 'Nothing to do there. No work. You can make enough here in a year to go home and live for two years. Anyway, I was sick of my husband. He used to beat me up. I wanted to stand on my own two feet. My parents are looking after my son.' 'What does your husband do?' She looks disgusted. 'Nothing. He's just a layabout. I don't know what he does now. I haven't seen him for months.' 'What are your plans?' 'Stay here, make some money, see if I can go back and set up a restaurant. There's decent money in that. What does the money look like in your country?' Foolishly, you draw out a ten pound note, and she holds it, and says 'I collect money. Can I have this?' Feeling slightly cheated, you nod. And then she moves even closer so you can feel her breath on your cheek as she speaks. 'This work is OK. Nothing else I can do. Just sit here with whoever chooses me.' You feel her breasts rub against you. 'Maybe you would like some other services. I can do good massage. What room are you in? Fifty dollars for one hour. A hundred, and I'll stay the night . Two hundred and I'll do anything.'*

The one stable point in Mao's ideology from the start of his intellectual career in the 1920s, to the end of it in 1976, was a commitment to the belief in the existence of set social classes. His collected works famously began with the lines from an essay in 1922, 'Who is our enemy. Who are our friends? This is the fundamental question'. And the answer was contained in class.

Marxism gave the impetus, but Mao's achievement was to translate that to the conditions in Chinese society in a way that was convincing and made sense. In later essays, he would meticulously classify the various social levels in the society around him – from comprador bourgeoisie to proletariat. Underlying this taxidermy was a moral dichotomy – between the good classes and the bad ones. The world was a site for Manichean struggle between the forces of proletariat and peasant right, and the darkness of the capitalists and landlords. The implementation of Mao's class beliefs in the 1950s led to the felling, and often death, of many thousands of those who belonged to the wrong side of the class tracks.

Part of the opening up and reform package has been that the Party has had to become rather more circumspect in what it says about class. And many of the people who have risen from the classless Utopia of Mao's later society look and act remarkably like the very people his political programme was meant to boot out eternally from the Chinese universe half a century before. There might not be warlords and landlords who can exercise the power over life and death the way they did in Republican China, but there are certainly local strongmen, people who are able to get away with extraordinary excesses, and operate very much like the power elite before 1949. It looks like the bad classes are back in force in the PRC of 2006.

A decade ago, a self-proclaimed dissident, who bore the scars from a beating administered to him during one of his encounters with over-zealous PSB (Public Security Bureau) officials, told me in a small restaurant in the town where I lived that class in China was simple to understand. Forget the multiple class descriptions supplied by Mao and his ideologues. Look at it, he said, as a three way split. There were the top- level, the officials, leaders, the elite. They lived in good housing, belonged deeply to the system, their kids and family were looked after, they had chauffeur driven cars, travelled first class wherever they went and stayed in the best hotels.

Then there was the middle class – university professors, teachers, doctors, some small business people and mid to lower level officials. They had reasonable benefits, a decent standard of life, and the hope of one day rising to the level above them. And then, he said, pausing for effect, there was the rubble. The people at the bottom. The peasants, the illiterate, the floating population, the workers. The very people, in fact, that Mao's revolution was meant to lift up.

In modern China, the poor are all around. Like in any sophisticated, large cities, the visible signs of poverty, in the centres, are becoming rarer – but their sporadic appearance can be all the more unsettling for occurring in such a materially rich context. Shenzhen serves up the most stomach churning example of this – a city constantly, frenetically, on the make, full of newcomers, bursting with entrepreneurial energy, where Mammon is worshipped on ever inch of tarmac, and where, somehow, 'the rubble' have managed to break through the checkpoints and walls separating this place from the rest of the PRC, appearing in the form of maimed beggars, dragging themselves along the pavement dressed in filthy, torn garments and country girls working as prostitutes walking along the sidewalks at night, offering themselves for a few yuan.

Contact with this army of the disenfranchised and rootless is necessarily limited for visitors. And yet, they are somehow there, just at the borders of vision, an unsettling, disturbing reminder that as the reform process has winners, the great economic juggernaut impressing the rest of the world has also left a record number of victims in its wake.

In 2005 alone, there were nearly a hundred thousand labour disputes in the PRC, many by workers laid of from slimmed down SOEs. Few of these got reported in the Chinese media. Those unceremoniously evicted from the iron rice bowl system, cradle to grave socialism, were left to find their own health, education and work welfare in a world where there were hundreds of millions of others in a similar predicament. The PRC's cities have filled up with marginal floating populations, mentioned in a previous chapter, who are regarded much like the menacing underclass in Victorian London, a sea of desperate faces that need to be kept at bay.

The underclass, the rabble, are like the chorus in a Greek tragedy, or the extras in a film. A backdrop, who critically intervene from time to time. The great mass that needs to be kept down, controlled, but where the final spark to start a prairie fire might come from. Popular rebellions are the ultimate bogeymen in Chinese politics, fellers of dynasties, sources of new elites and emperors.

Looking at the hordes of the underclass as they prepare for their annual journey back to their home towns over Chinese new year from the PRC's great urban train stations, it is hard to imagine that any new leadership might be milling around here though. Underclasses are rarely given the privilege of being able to congregate together. They are kept in whatever ghettoes they might be able to construct and find in the places where they have come to seek for work. Only at times like this do they ever come together in any volume, and give an idea of their enormity. At these times, Beijing Station, now a true Soviet style monument stranded amongst new glistening tower blocks and wide roads becomes an island from another era – a temple to the workers and proletariat, its sole refuge for outsiders being the 'VIP ticket office', a somewhat redundant place now you can book train tickets online, but still one of the final spots in Beijing where you can catch a whiff of the old Maoist style country – and also fondly remember the comforts it offered even only a decade ago when access to it granted real privileges.

The great irony supplied by the cast of characters constituting contemporary PRC is that the underclass are also the greatest weapon that the country has – the source of its plentiful cheap labour which has given it the competitive advantage over other manufacturing countries, and made it, in former Premier Zhu Rongji's somewhat excited words, the factory of the world. According to Mao, the more Chinese there were the better. He famously shocked his advisers by once suggesting that the PRC has nothing to fear from a nuclear attack. If it lost half its population, it would still have more than most other countries. Mao's enthusiastic support for big families was to be criticized even by his most fervent admirers as his greatest error. A joke told to me in Beijing by a lawyer captures this. Bill Clinton, Boris Yeltsin and Jiang Zemin are travelling on a train. When Clinton saw a problem, being an American, he drew out a wad of money and chucked it out of the window. When Yeltsin saw a problem, he said he would give up half of Siberia to help out. Jiang Zemin just sighed and said he'd no money and not much land, but here, have a few million people. 'We won' t even notice they've gone.'

That enormous population still makes the eyes of most western business people glaze over. One Chinese person buying your drink, or your clothes, and you and your children and your children's children need never work again. A billion consumers is the most powerful aphrodisiac for any entrepreneur. And promoters of such figures don't take kindly to someone pointing out that a vast number of these are still desperately poor. For the resources and power they contain, they also offer the most massive challenges. And even when they all rise up to a standard of living modestly comparable to the west, the problems don't stop – they just change. The PRC's population with the car usage of a country like the UK (half the number of cars as there are actual people), without highly green fuel options, would effectively signal the death knell for the planet's environment. If Chinese consumers become anywhere near as voracious as their American and European counterparts, there will be little of the planet left.

So while one might marvel at the economic power of the new elite, and listen in fascinated silence to the tales of intrigue, woe and complexity of the intellectuals – and be knocked back by the beauty, energy and driving ambition of the legion of Little Miss Wangs, for real raw power, one must look to the underclass. Like a mighty river, when confined within its banks, an object that impresses and amazes. But once unleashed, uncontrollable and terrifying, the least known, least understood, least noticed part of the Chinese human landmass, and the one that is most critical for its future stability and global integration.

CONCLUSION:
MANY CHINAS, MANY TRUTHS

The price of globalization and internationalization seems to be that the boundaries change every five minutes. Once we get used to one way of looking at things, then another new set of ideas front up – some repackaged from older ones, some wholly novel. We seem to be like the characters from Lewis Caroll's *Alice Through the Looking Glass*, furiously chasing into a reflection of ourselves, doomed to never quite catch up no matter how much effort we expend.

Those who cast their eyes over the way we talk, think and write about the PRC in the twenty-first century might be forgiven for thinking we need a whole new vocabulary in order to talk about what we see and what is happening. This is a two-way problem. The PRC's language about itself has hardly changed over the years and decades. Still pooh-facedly describing itself as a 'Marxist-Leninist' one party state, while the world outside implodes in commercial chaos cum euphoria, forcing us to end up with paradoxes like 'market led socialism'. Outside, we are still hung up on the language of outsiders. We can either hint at an intimate respect or relationship with the inner workings of this elephantine regime, or throw our very best antipathy at it. Either way, we are doomed to be locating ourselves inside, or outside, the solid Great Mental Wall.

This book has looked thematically at some of the areas where the paradigm of talking and thinking about the PRC most definitely needs to be thought about. And first we should look long and hard at the very term 'China' and decide more precisely what we mean by it. China as it exists now could be described as an empire, a confederation, a region, a country. But the tensions and contradictions that exist within this entity are very stark. I've opted for the very deliberate term 'PRC' simply because the PRC as it exists now has major differences with previous Chinas that have existed, in terms of geography, political structure, and composition. This China has a history that is different from the Chinas before. And it will have an impact and role in the future that will be different from theirs. The first lesson of looking at the current entity, the PRC, is that while certain bits of history do need to be looked at, some need to be either ignored, or pushed into the background. We need to get much better at spotting similarities and differences.

China All Change

This issue of continuity and discontinuity in China and the PRC's recent and ancient history is a fascinating one. One can draw strange and interesting parallels between the Chinas of the past, and what happened in them, and the China that exists now and is called the PRC. The CR, for instance, which I argued was one of the seminal moments in the formation of the PRC and the consciousness of its contemporary citizens, has linkages, of a sort, with the Literary Inquisition, set up the Qianlong Emperor in the eighteenth century. His 'burning of books' left less of an imprint in society, but this agitation against the intelligentsia, and attempt to redraw society's cultural boundaries was something repeated, with vengeance, two centuries later. Far from being a unique aberration, the CR at least had antecedents in some of its aspects.

This works down to the history within the PRC. The great divide between before and after 1978, and the Party Congress that started off the Reform and Opening up Process, while it has a pleasing dramatic edge to it, needs to be questioned. Many of the aspirations of the post-1978 period were articulated before that date – the idea, for instance, that the PRC would overtake the UK in steel production, which had been one of the abiding dreams behind the fiasco of the Great Leap Forward from 1957 to 1958. The difference between the great modernization and development ambitions of the 1950s and 1970s and 1980s was simply that one means was used to promote one, and another, more successful means to push forward the other. The aspiration was the same. China's first Great Leap Forward has manifested itself again in its second, longer and much more powerful Leap Forward, a leap continuing to this day.

This plotting of similarities works in many other areas. The creation of a civil society in the PRC, for instance, has been one of the major preoccupations for those inside and outside the PRC for the last quarter of a century. When would the PRC's strong state institutions allow for non-government organizations, for instance – and freedom for citizens to set up interest groups with an agenda separate from the Party and the State? But as Qiushe Ma argues in a recent study, NGO's existed deep into the Qing Dynasty, and indeed, thrived in the early years of the Republican Period. Religious societies, foreign NGOs, Chinese business associations, cultural organizations, all of them had a vibrant life in the 1920s and 1930s, cut short by first war and then the great PRC project. NGO life died in the 1950s and 1960s, but paradoxically, as the central state has pulled away from providing services it once used to, in areas like health care, education, and poverty relief, NGOs have sprung up and stepped in. The monolithic Chinese state, in fact, has proved itself simply unable to supply the sort of 'cradle to grave' iron rice bowl services it once did. And this has been an opportunity for non-state entities to develop.

The PRC was different from the Chinese entities that existed before. In some ways, events over the last 60 years have followed a vast parabola. One could argue that we have ended up where we started – with the same return to regionalist tensions of the 1920s and 30s, the same unbridled corruption, the same weak central state, and interfering outsiders slowly increasing their involvement. Some, like UK academic Rana Mitter, would even argue that the KMT government was well on its way to launching a true prototype of the internationalised Chinese state being constructed today. War and invasion prevented this getting very far, but the signs were there.[1] The great PRC projects of the first 40 years after 1949 were aberrations. So were the strident declarations of nationalism associated with them. What we are witnessing now, and have been for over two decades, is a face saving way of admitting that, despite their heroism and noble intentions, the revolutionary immortals were, in fact, wrong. The 'real' China, hovering behind the PRC, is coming back into existence – and it, like its predecessors, was disunited, unstable, contained extremes of wealth and poverty, and was easy prey for foreign intervention.

But...

History might have patterns, but it rarely photocopies itself. The PRC now has several major advantages. It has nuclear weapons, it has unified institutions like the Party and the Army, and it has globalization. It is not in the world's interests to see a disunited failing China – especially as its economy becomes more and more integrated, and its contacts beyond its border deepen. Everyone has too much to lose from a fall. While we need to think differently about what 'China' is, and what it might become, we don't need to rub our hands at the idea of it tumbling into chaos and disunity. That would send waves over us all – and create an international economic 'tsunami' that would flood areas far beyond our beaches.

---

1 Rana Mitter, *A Bitter Revolution*, Oxford 2004.

Part of our problem is the level of knowledge about the PRC. Someone commented recently that the average Chinese person knows far more about the West than Westerners do about China. There are far more speakers of English, far more people who have links or visited the West, and far more news about the west than there is in, for instance, the UK about China.. While there is increasing exposure of Chinese in UK media, that doesn't equate to any meaningful expertise. Barely 300 graduates a year study Chinese in the UK. There are only a handful of universities that offer Mandarin Chinese as a subject. Durham University recently took the depressing decision of closing down its East Asian Studies Department, despite its being one of the oldest in the UK, simply because the student-teacher ratios in Mandarin tuition made the courses run at high losses. While some secondary schools do offer Mandarin A Levels, they are few and far between. In the twenty-first century, while the PRC grows in prominence and importance, we have barely enough linguists to man a large conference.

And while there is a huge amount of material published on the PRC, very little of it reaches the mainstream. There are dozens of specialist publications, and excellent academic studies, produced each year. But the readership for these is limited. There are few decent approachable studies of Chinese history, Chinese culture and Chinese politics. Discourse about the PRC in the UK at least resides in two extremes – highly academic, or hopelessly oversimplified. The enormous audience for Jung Chang's *Wild Swans* for instance was probably attracted by the book confirming their assumptions about China, rather than offering any new knowledge about the place. Julia Lovell's *Great Wall of China* offers a far richer starting point.

Indeed, scratching the surface, one wonders how much people might want to know about the new China they are seeing so much about on TV and in the papers. We might be compared to residents in a city wholly clueless to the deluge of new people suddenly flooding its gates. Do they offer a challenge? An opportunity? Are they a threat? Do they have benign or hostile intent? Where are they similar to us? Where different? This simple menu of questions seems lacking in most discussions about the PRC. On the whole, people seem content with the old parameters – they like the idea of a China of introspection, abuse, human rights problems, people on bicycles, the Great Wall visible from the moon and the other sundry myths, half truths and simplifications that make up the popular picture of what China is. Maintaining these in the face of the entity that the PRC is becoming is like still believing that miniature people within the radio are what causes the voices.

We are lucky that so many people originally from mainland China have come over to many American and British universities in the last two decades. The work they have produced has offered an excellent basis for dialogue and communication. The number of scholars going the other way, however, has been limited. The grim fact remains that, at the start of the twenty-first century, with China impacting on our environment, society and global commerce more than ever before, we are ill equipped to understand both what it as a country stands for, and how to take our dialogue forward. In many ways, we have outsourced this requirement to Chinese who have migrated here, or to Hong Kong or other Chinese areas – on the highly questionable assumption that ethnicity alone is the basis for being able to interpret one culture to another.

The history of predictions is as long as history proper. Playing the 'what will happen next game' goes back to prehistory. But it is odd how little we look back over recent predictions, and see where they were right and wrong. In the mid 1990s, for instance, few predicted that within a decade the PRC's energy usage would become the issue it has. Some predicted that the current system would implode at some point, and another Tiananmen would occur. Some saw the PRC becoming a place of sinister intent, working on its military in order to grab parcels of territory, especially Taiwan. The PRC's problems were considered far too grave to be easily resolved in the next decade or so.

We were right back then about the grave crisis facing the PRC's environment – and despite the planting of something like a billion trees north of Beijing, that crisis has not got much better. The Olympics were seen by some as a boost to the PRC's environment protection – but as I argued above, the environment in some areas has got far worse. The imperatives for commerce and development are still held out up front. The PRC's desire to become a world class player in some areas has made for a more proactive engagement policy – but this has been largely guided by self-interest rather than principle, and on many issues the PRC remains fiercely anti-interventionist. Improvement in the rule of law, human rights, and issues like press freedom have ebbed and flowed, but few would say that these are significantly better than the mid 1990s. The one big change is simply that the aspiring Chinese middle class have grown economically much freer, and are granted liberties that would have been hard to foresee a decade back. In this area, the PRC has indeed changed. The citizens of the PRC are deeply divided, but to those in the right camp, however large or small (there is debate about whether the county's new middle class is 50 million strong, or 150 million, or a quarter of a billion) have more freedom than their parents and grandparents did. The PRC still remains a society that has a power elite. And that power elite continues to protect its powers as much as possible. But as tax payment levels show, the Chinese state is not the all-encompassing beast it once was. And there are wide swathes of areas of activity where people may do as they please.

Remember, Never Enter the Zone

The Zone, the area of sensitivity, has boundaries that shift and change. But at its heart lie two unquestionables. The legitimacy of the Party to continue, unchallenged, in power, And the right of the PRC to assert its monopoly over expressions or articulations of Chinese interest. Touching these leads to problems, just as it did in 1995. The situation now, and for the foreseeable future, is a delicate balance. People will continue to be allowed freedoms, and will enjoy and develop those. But there will be increasing tensions for them to participate more in the decisions which influence their daily lives. Complaints about corruption and nepotism will continue, but unless these reach a critical mass, they alone will not be enough to sink the current status quo. That would take a mixture of internal and external forces – natural disasters, unhelpful foreign interference and economic downturns. If these come along, the PRC's days may well be numbered, and its replacement a group of states rather than one single one, with a somewhat fractious relationship with each other, not just a fanciful possibility but a real likelihood.

That is unlikely – at the moment – but not unthinkable. The faultlines of the PRC are deep, as previous chapters have shown – and while there is strength in unity at the moment, it is not impossible that the great booming coastal provinces might start to resent the drag on their commercial and social development by the inland provinces. Never underestimate the disunity that lurks beneath the fervently asserted unity. The shadow of the warlord period might then return once more.

What is almost certain, more certain than any other prediction one could make, is that the PRC, or whatever China or China's that might exist in the future, will matter for those outside more than ever before. China is coming to a place near us, disproving the old image of the introspective, inward looking Chinese behind their mythical great wall. If this was ever true (and in many ways, it was a myth built by people both sides) it is being disproved by the day now. In sheer size, economic aspirations, number of people, impact on the environment, nothing has been seen like the current PRC. To have a lifestyle even approaching the one we have grown used to in the West would be to place almost unthinkable burdens on the world's environment. But to continue to expect Chinese not to aspire in increasing numbers to this sort of lifestyle is also unlikely. We, and the PRC, will interact more and more as the years go on – our dialogue will become more and more complicated. We will need to know more about each other, have different ways of talking about each other and understanding each other. Relying on specialization will no longer do. We need to see Chinese studies enter the mainstream. And we need to ensure that we have control of parts of the agenda between our two cultures. That is the final responsibility of seeing the PRC come to be a China not only close to us, but in many ways a China in whose world we live, in whose shadow we need to carve out our own space and in whose future we are not just interested bystanders, but direct stakeholders, with our own critical interests to articulate, and, more often than not, defend.

A POLEMICAL BIBLIOGRAPHY

The mountain of books about China grows higher by the year. There are journals, guides, monographs, excellent and comprehensive websites, produced in all corners of the world. What follows is a deeply subjective, and highly partial, suggested list for that endangered species, the general reader who has not, so far, read a great deal about China. This might also offer to the many other communities interested and engaged with China a more exotic path through the bibliographic jungle. These books listed below, while I don't argue contain the finest and best scholarship, are ones that helped me navigate, and provoked thoughts, about the conflicting feelings that encountering contemporary China raised in me over the last decade and a half.

The most exciting, and best presented, book about contemporary China is the weighty volume edited by Harvard Professor of Architecture (and, currently, designer of one of the more striking additions to the Beijing skyline) Rem Koolhaas, *Great Leap Forward* (Taschen, GMBH 2001). *Great Leap Forward* has the huge advantage of using many excellent photos and images to back up its provocative arguments. It also presents China as a subject of interest, and available to critical thinking, as any other more mundane, traditionally accessible environment. Tracking fresher and more original thinking about China back a few decades, one could do far worse than look at the four tomes written from the late 1960s to the early 1980s by Belgian Pierre Ryckmans, going under the pseudonym Simon Leys. *Chinese Shadows* (London, 1978), first published in French in 1974 contains a hilarious tourist chapter around Late Maoism ('Follow the Guide'), which was the inspiration for the tour of the Dark Side of the Chinese Economy contained in Chapter 5. Simon Leys's account, however, carries a far more serious and weightier register. *Broken Images* (London, 1979), and *The Chairman's New Clothes* (London, 1969) contain further delicately ironic insights. While time may have moved on, now and again rereading Leys's works one has a terrible sense that the China he is writing about is still very clearly visible, beneath the sheen of new buildings and character types populating the landscape.

Anyone interested in working out the path taken by the political dispossessed and dissenters from 1970 onwards can study the excellent anthology *Seeds of Fire* (Newcastle, 1989), put together after the great events of 1989 by Geremie Barmie and John Minford. This book is made all the more poignant by the subsequent let-down of some of its most powerful voices. Dissident Wei Jingsheng, especially, whose fiery description of the prison for political prisoners in Beijing, and demand for greater democracy were produced before his release to the west, has subsequently pursued an abrasive career which has proved to be an anti-climax. Another delightful moment is perhaps one of the first debunkings translated into English of the myth of the saintly Zhou Enlai, a figure now well and truly implicated with all the various henchmen and collaborators around him for the disasters of Late Maoism – and perhaps better seen as Chairman Mao's willing executioner.

Hong Kong based academic Xiaoyang Wang seems to be the only person to have written convincingly about the moral transformations wrecked on the PRC by the rapid development and 'opening up' of the last few decades. Her 'The Post Communist Personality' (issued in *The China Journal*, January 2002) provides a wholly new framework to look at the sort of journey the Chinese have travelled from late Maoist absolutism to the current market relativist pragmatism.

Books about the economic developments of China in the last quarter century proliferate every year. The works by Cambridge Professor of Chinese Management (the first such position in the world) Peter Nolan, and the *China Dream* by Joe Studwell (London and New York, 2002) contain more than enough food for thought about the current idiosyncrasies of the Chinese Economic miracle. Nolan's take on the general weakness of Chinese companies compared to western style ones, and the reasons behind this, can be found in, among other works, *China and the Global Economy* (London, 2001). Studwell's rather more practical work recounts the various great expectations, and then sudden nasty shocks and downfalls, of the many foreign business people who have gone to China to make their millions. Both Nolan and Studwell offer plenty of antidotes to the fatal proclivity of outsiders to either be utterly dismissive of what the Chinese economy offers, or become hopeless Panglosses.

In terms of sensible works about the CR, beyond highly academic books, there are few attractive access points. Michael Schoenhals's *China's Cultural Revolution, 1966–1969: Not a Dinner Party* (New York and London, 1996) despite its racy title, offers excerpts from the main documents of the period – one of the most haunting being the transcripts of the public humiliation and struggle session against Liu Shaoqi's wife, Wang Guangmei (who, unlike her husband, survived this period to be rehabilitated and work as a member of the National People's Congress after 1978.) Nien Cheng's *Life and Death in Shanghai* (New York, 1986) is probably the best individual narrative in English of one of the many 'persecuted' in the CR. Nien was an executive for Shell in Shanghai, and therefore an immediate target once the revolution had been kicked off. Parts of her account are deeply moving. A red-hot recent addition is the comprehensive history of the CR put together over many years by Schoenhals and MacFarquhar.

Mobo Gao has dealt with other more sensationalist accounts of the CR period in his essay in the *Bulletin of Concerned Asian Scholars*, No 27, 'Memoirs and Interpretations of the CR' and 'Debating the Cultural Revolution: Do We Only Know What We Believe' (*Critical Asian Studies*, No 34). His summary dismissal of the hugely popular *Wild Swans* by Jun Chang is particularly sweet – rather like her more recent biography of Mao, her account is riddled with overstatement, and contradictions that would please the great Master of Contradiction himself, Mao. These pallid works should be held against the great *A Cadre Life in Six Chapters* (Hong Kong, 1982) by Yang Jiang, a work both brief, deeply ironic, and, in the words of Simon Leys, conveying as much real despair and anguish in one sentence as most books do in a hundred pages. Ba Jin's *Random Thoughts* (Hong Kong, 1984) contains similarly powerful and succinct recollections of the 'holocaust' – but this from the more physically comfortable, and less spiritually reassuring, viewpoint of someone who had suffered relatively lightly during this period, but lived to reflect with deep regret on it, and voiced that literally for a whole generation. The more complete works are readily available in Chinese as *Sui Xiang Lu*.

Mao Zedong is a tough subject to broach. Books about him divide into overt hagiography (the earlier accounts), or total hatchet jobs (the latest). Li Zhisui, having been Mao's personal physician for so long, had the best access, and his *The Private Life of Chairman Mao*, (published in English by Chatto and Windus, 1994) was heartily condemned by the Beijing government of the time, who were left to rue their leniency in letting Dr Li go off to the US a few years earlier, sure he would never spill what beans he knew. Despite accounts of Mao's general lack of hygiene, and his lifelong proclivity to interpret his phrase 'women hold up half the sky' by demanding a stream of country girls to his large, custom made bed (though it is hard to reconcile this with the book strewn mess that Li describes elsewhere – like Churchill and Stalin, Mao was a creature of the night and seldom functioned during the day) Mao comes across in this exhaustive account as being beguilingly human. He certainly had the capacity to connect with people around him and inspire their affection in a way it is hard to discern in any of the accounts of interaction by others with Stalin.

Mao's words were polished and tidied by the finest editors. The unexpurgated versions occur in Stuart Schram's *Mao Tse-tung Unrehearsed* (Harmondsworth, 1974) and more sensationally in Roderick MacFarquhar *et al, The Secret Speeches of Chairman Mao* (Harvard, 1989). The Mao of the latter, when not cursing and reminiscing, comes across as a rambling old man in his dotage. It is easy after reading these books to appreciate the contribution of his propagandists to the great image of Mao that was subsequently created.

Books about the use and interpretation of Chinese language, especially political language, are few and far between. Ping Chen's *Modern Chinese: History and Sociolingustics* (Cambridge, 1999) is a brave and straightforward attempt. Michael Schoenhals's *Doing Things with Words in Chinese Politics* (Berkeley, 1992) takes texts from the first three decades of the PRC's existence, and analyses them, mostly through the application of Speech Act philosophy. My own *The Purge of the Inner Mongolian People's Party in the Cultural Revolution in China, 1967–1969* (London, 2006) despite its cumbersome title (bequeathed from the PhD thesis it was based on) uses more general discourse theory to look at CR documents – though this could quite easily be applied to later political documents.

There are, of course, the great and monumental works of Chinese scholarship. *The Cambridge Histories of China*, the continuing project begun by the greatest European sinologist of the last century, Joseph Needham, of *The Science and Civilisation in China* series, a work that reminds us how much our current culture owes to the East, and now being edited by the excellent Christopher Cullen, one of the few who combines deep knowledge of science and Chinese history and culture to the standards attained and expected by the founder of this project.

In terms of literary accounts, however, there is, strangely, only one account by a foreigner of any real merit, the *China Trilogy* by Christopher New, published by Asia 2000 (Hong Kong, 2002). New's middle volume, in particular, *The China Box*, with its sombre tale of an academic in Hong Kong's tragic involvement with a mainland refugee might be called the generic story of these myriad mismatches between Westerners and Easterners. Like many of the works above, this one has the great advantage of being brief.

INDEX